W9-AOB-619

OVERDUE FINES ARE 25¢ PER DAY
ITEM

84 P 11.00
cat

Blacks in Suburbs

Blacks in Suburbs

A National Perspective

Thomas A. Clark

with a foreword by

George Sternlieb

RUTGERS UNIVERSITY
CENTER FOR URBAN POLICY RESEARCH
NEW BRUNSWICK, NEW JERSEY

Thomas A. Clark is an assistant professor of urban policy planning and policy development at Rutgers University and a research associate of Rutger's Center for Urban Policy Research. He is currently engaged in research regarding urban economic development, dependent populations in cities, regional policy, and capital flows in interregional linkage networks.

E
185.89
.H6
C56

Cover design by Francis G. Mullen

Copyright 1979, Rutgers—The State University of New Jersey
All rights reserved

Published in the United States of America
by the Center for Urban Policy Research
Building 4051—Kilmer Campus
New Brunswick, New Jersey 08903

Library of Congress Cataloging in Publication Data

Clark, Thomas A   1944-
    Blacks in suburbs, a national perspective.

    Bibliography: p.
    1. Afro-Americans—Housing. 2. Afro-Americans—
Economic conditions. 3. Afro-Americans—Social conditions—
1964-1975. 4. Afro-Americans—Social conditions—1975-
5. Suburbs—United States. 6. Migration, Internal—United
States. I. Title.
E185.89.H6C56   330.9'73   79-12171
ISBN 0-88285-061-X

to my parents

Contents

List of Exhibits

Exhibit

Foreword

Black Americans are slowly and painfully beginning to replicate the settlement patterns of the white immigrant in America: from farm to city slum and then for a select number, the suburb. The process imperfect at best, is beset still by many degrees of uncertainty and by racial discrimination; it is hindered by poverty for many and, as always, held back by insecurity about the future. But for blacks of the middle class, at least, suburbanization is taking place and at an increasing rate.

The implications of this process are monumental. It does not mean that the issue of racial prejudice will be laid to rest. The millenium is not at hand. Increasingly however, the problem replacing racism will be the hard rocks of class structure and income inadequacy. Responding to these issues is well within our immediate competence; it is to be seen whether such responses are within our national will.

What does suburbanization really mean? In the context of black outmigration, does it not really involve shifts outside of the archaic central city limits but to residence immediately peripheral? That, at best would involve only marginal improvement, given the aging of the inner suburb. How does black suburbanization fit into the wave of exurbanization which dominates new development subject only to the availability of gasoline? Can the new wave of black suburbanites use homeownership as the super Christmas Club, a preferred form of leveraged forced saving and as a repository of stored capital, successfully replicating the experience of their white predecessors?

This study conducted by Professor Thomas Clark is the first in a series of publications which takes up these and related issues. The Center for Urban Policy Research is attempting to pursue, describe and clarify the dynamics of the migration, of the institutions and the barriers at work in the process. We are deeply grateful to the Department of Health, Education and Welfare for making this possible— and to Professor Clark for a firm statistical foundation as an essential first step.

George Sternlieb

Acknowledgments

This national perspective on black suburbanization is funded under a grant to the Center for Urban Policy Research, Rutgers University from the Public Health Service, National Institute of Mental Health, U.S. Department of Health, Education and Welfare (Grant Number MH31324-02). The larger purpose of the grant is to examine the institutional factors affecting the scope, pace and form of black suburbanization. Dr. George Sternlieb serves as the Principal Investigator for the several phases of research regarding this larger objective, while Professor Robert Lake is the Project Manager. I am indebted to both for their assistance and encouragement throughout this phase of research. Thanks are also due the staff at the Center for Urban Policy Research for its work supporting this effort. Mr. Dan Sohmer has been particularly helpful in overseeing the various stages of preparation on the way to final publication. My wife, Diana, deserves special thanks for her forbearance and support.

Blacks in Suburbs

1

Introduction

Over one-ninth of the American population is black, and one in three blacks lives in poverty. Still more live on the fringes of poverty. In a nation commanding such wealth it is not merely provocative but essential to consider why this magnitude of deprivation exists. If the rate of black poverty were shared by the American population at large, then an explanation would have to be sought in the general national processes which produce and distribute wealth. The rate of black poverty, however, is three times as great as for non-blacks. Less than one-tenth of the white population, itself diverse, lives in poverty. An explanation for black poverty must therefore be sought not only in the general configuration of the national economic process but also in the panoply of conditions unique to this racial minority.

Today, three-quarters of the black population lives in metropolitan areas with the remainder living in the rural regions and smaller towns and cities of nonmetropolitan America.[1] Of those residing in metropolitan areas, four in five live in central cities. In the central cities having the largest black populations, most blacks reside within high density poverty areas.[2] In some central cities there also exist significant enclaves of middle and even upper income dwellings, many of which are occupied by black households. In addition, in 1977, 4.6 million blacks resided in metropolitan areas, outside central cities.

This black suburban population has almost doubled since 1960 and today constitutes six percent of the entire suburban population within metropolitan areas.[3]

Perceived Roles of Black Suburbanization

If black residential patterns reveal the condition of the black community at large, changes in these patterns in time often reveal its aspirations. No dynamic of black demography has more often been cited in this regard than that of black surburbanization. "Black suburbanization", the absolute increase in the number of blacks living in suburbs, is commonly regarded as a measure of social and economic advance. For this there are perhaps three reasons. First, it is often asserted that blacks who have achieved substantial income and wealth will exercise their prosperity by moving to the suburbs. Second, it is argued that as less prosperous blacks relocate in low and moderate income housing in suburbs, they acquire a superior environment in which to raise families, educate their children, and pursue employment opportunities.[4] For these, suburban residence is perceived to be a helpful assist up the socio-economic ladder. Of course, as blacks gain greater geographical assess to suburban "resources" including homes and jobs, spatial discrimination may give way to other forms of social, economic, and political exclusion. This would tend to negate the positive effect of black suburbanization, which must ultimately be conceived not only as a spatial but also an institutional process. Third, some argue that without the dispersal of central city poverty populations into suburbs it will be impossible to revitalize the nation's central cities.[5] Others counter that black suburban dispersal would diminish the political voice of the black community in central cities.[6]

In any event, not all residential areas to which prosperous blacks might be drawn are "suburban". High quality residential opportunities exist not only in many nonmetropolitan areas, but also in most if not all central cities. In addition, less prosperous blacks often can improve their residential setting without moving to the suburbs, nor need dispersal from central cities cease at the perimeter of the metropolitan area. Black suburbanization, it seems, is not the only means *for* or index *of* improvement in the socio-economic status of the black population.

Black Residential Patterns in Suburbs: A Typology. To a large extent, the kind of suburban community to which blacks move will determine the meaning for them of "suburbanization". And today, though many live inter-mixed within predominantly white communities, still larger numbers in many metropolitan areas reside in predominantly black inner-ring *spillover communities* adjacent to the central city, and *outlying racial enclaves*.[7] These enclaves may be either *newly emergent* or *pre-metropolitan*. The former may arise through a process of white-to-black racial succession focused on incipient nodes of racial turnover, or they may take the form of newer residential development.[8] The densities of these newer developments will tend to identify the income structure of their residents, so they encompass a spectrum of types. The latter, "pre-metropolitan" communities, are those that once functioned in relative isolation before being encircled by the expanding metropolitan region.

Overview of the Book

Rapid black suburbanization is a relatively recent phenomenon. Indeed, the pace has quickened appreciably since the last national census. In addition there is clear evidence that the mix of types of black households seeking to reside in the suburbs has changed as blacks have begun in increasing numbers to rise up the economic ladder. The black middle class, which just several decades ago was very small in relation to the black population at large, is now far more significant. And it is today a major participant in the move to the suburbs. Joining it, of course, are additional numbers of less prosperous black households whose range of suburban residential options is far more limited.

Clearly, black suburbanization is not a monolithic process, but rather several distinct but interrelated avenues of movement distinguished by the nature, mix and pace of migration to the suburbs, as well as the identity, pattern and receptiveness of the suburban communities to which black migrations are directed. But while considerable work has been done to identify the spatial configuration of black suburban residences in particular metropolitan areas, less has been done to articulate the structure of these distinct classes of migration. Without a more precise knowledge of these classes it will remain difficult to assess existing public policies associated with black welfare and suburbanization, or to characterize the significance of black movement to the suburbs, or to chart a workable future course for public policy.

This book seeks to fill a void in the literature regarding the recent national dimensions of the movement of blacks to suburbs. It is to provide an initial impetus in developing a more textured understanding of the several distinct processes which have been too freely joined together in the concept of "black suburbanization". Chapter 2 considers the opposing forces which *propel* and *inhibit* the movement of blacks to suburbs, and how the resolution of these contradictory forces shapes the outcome. Chapter 3 documents the origins, characteristics and conditions of the black population now residing in the nation's suburbs. Recent trendlines are presented in the context of the massive shifts now reordering the demographic balance among regions, between central cities and suburbs, and between metropolitan and nonmetropolitan areas. The aggregate national perspective, of course, is a composite picture which may conceal important differences in the nature of black suburbanization among the major subnational regions. Chapter 4 therefore examines interregional differences in the shape and pace of change in the black suburban population. In fact, significant differences are discovered which reflect the distinctive geographic histories of these regions, and which challenge us to develop still greater sensitivity to the nuances of the process.

Chapter 5 selects certain major metropolitan areas for closer investigation. This Chapter examines several distinct hypotheses regarding black suburbanization and in doing so provides further insight into the great diversity among areas. Chapter 6 explicitly considers black suburbanization as a spatial process driven by selective migration from diverse origins. It explores the myth of black suburbanization as a one-way process, and documents the important functional linkages among race, migration and welfare. Chapter 7 focuses on black suburban poverty and employment potentials. It further examines the reality of the "hidden poor" who reside in suburbs, and discusses the geographic and institutional barriers that govern the pursuit of employment and the advancement of careers.

Blacks seeking to reside in suburbs inevitably must jockey for position in two distinct but closely related markets: labor and housing. The individual household may in fact reposition itself several times in each market before reaching an acceptable reconciliation. And over the life-span of the household a succession of subsequent adjustments may be necessary to accomodate changing conditions and opportunities. Chapter 8 considers the interaction between the markets for housing and labor within the *joint search space* of the individual household. In particular, it considers the character of dwellings occupied by suburban households, their relative competitiveness in central city and suburban markets, and their assessment of both the dwellings and the neighborhoods they currently occupy. In addition, black-white differentials in suburban housing are examined. A concluding Chapter examines the degree to which *class* may supplant *race* in governing suburban prospects.

NOTES

1. These figures pertain to the United States Census Bureau's "Standard Metropolitan Statistical Areas" or "SMSA's", each of which contains one central city having at least 50,000 people, or two central cities, neither having fewer than 15,000, whose combined population is at least 50,000, plus surrounding counties determined to relate to the central city according to serveral interaction criteria.

2. In 1970, 26 cities had black populations in excess of 100,000. In all but three of these cities the majority of blacks lived in higher density, low income areas designated by the U.S. Census Bureau. These "poverty areas" include all census tracts in which at least 20 percent of the population was below the poverty level in 1969. The exceptions were Washington, D.C., Detroit, and Indianapolis.

3. U.S. Bureau of the Census, *Current Population Reports*, "Social and Economic Characteristics of Metropolitan and Non-Metropolitan Areas, 1977 and 1970," Series P-23, No. 75 (Washington, D.C.: U.S. Government Printing Office, November, 1978).

4. John Kain, in particular argues that high black unemployment rates in metropolitan areas are due primarily to suburban housing discrimination that denies blacks access to suburban jobs. See John F. Kain, "Housing Segregation, Negro Employment and Metropolitan Decentralization," *Quarterly Journal of Economics*, Vol. 82 (1968), 175-197.

5. This argument is advanced most forcefully by Anthony Downs, *Opening Up the Suburbs* (New Haven: Yale University Press, 1973). Bennett Harrison, however, believes central city economic development is both feasible and desirable, and that black dispersal is neither a necessary nor at all times a desirable prerequisite. Bennett Harrison, *Urban Economic Development: Suburbanization, Minority Opporitunity and the Condition of the Central City* (Washington, D.C.: The Urban Institute, 1974). See also, Nathan Glazer, "On 'Opening Up' the Suburbs," *Public Interest*, Vol. 37 (1974), 89-111. In any case, the beneficiaries of central city revitalization will be determined largely by the method in which revitalization is pursued. Gentrification may in fact hasten the dispersal of many low and even moderate income households to the suburbs and beyond. The result may be substantially increased pressure especially on the older, inner suburbs to accommodate additonal numbers of blacks. These suburbs may well become functional if not political extensions of the central city.

6. See, for example, Norman Fainstein and Susan Fainstein, *Urban Political Movements: The Search for Power by Minority Groups in American Cities* (Englewood Cliffs, New Jersey: Prentice Hall, 1974), J. David Greenstone and Paul E. Peterson, *Race and Authority in Urban Politics: Community Participation and the War on Poverty* (New York: Russell Sage Foundation, 1973), and Frances Fox Piven and Richard A. Cloward, "Black Control of Cities," *The New Republic*, September 30 and October 7, 1967. See also, M.N. Danielson, "Differentiation, Segregation and Political Fragmentation in the American Metropolis," in *Governance and Population*, edited by A.E.K. Nash (Washington, D.C.: Commission on Population Growth and the American Future, Research Reports, Vol. 4,

1972), 143-76, and H. Paul Friesma, "Black Control of Central Cities: The Hollow Prize," *Journal of the American Institute of Planners*, Vol. 35 (1965), 75-9.

7. Harold M. Rose identifies two classes of emergent black suburban communities: "spillover," from prior ghetto areas and "black colonies". Harold M. Rose, *Black Suburbanization: Access to Improved Quality of Life or Maintenance of the Status Quo?* (Cambridge, Massachusetts: Ballinger, 1976).

8. Reynolds Farley distinguishes three types of suburban areas experiencing black suburbanization: older communities undergoing racial succession, newer developments conceived for blacks, and other enclaves of impoverished black households. Reynolds Farley, "The Changing Distribution of Negroes within Metropolitan Areas: The Emergence of Black Suburbs," *American Journal of Sociology*, Vol. 75 (1970), 512-529.

2

Propulsive and Exclusionary Factors in Black Suburban Entry

Forces Accelerating Black Suburbanization

Whatever the "purpose", significance or effect of black suburbanization, its causes are reasonably clear. First, the civil rights movement and the Great Society programs of the 1960's as well as the general strength of the national economy have led to a significant narrowing of the black-white income gap since 1960.[1] One major impetus in this convergence has been the rapid increase in black college enrollment.[2] In 1955, black men working full time earned less than two-thirds the average income of their white counterparts. By 1975, their earned income was 77 percent that of white men. In this same period the income of black women working full time rose from 57 to 99 percent that of white women. Many blacks, of course, are under- or unemployed so these gap percentages would be lower for the working force at large.[3] Still, today, more than one in four black families receive $15,000 or more in annual income. The number of black households which can afford to rent or purchase suburban homes is now greater than at any earlier time though housing costs have risen substantially, reducing purchasing power even as incomes have increased.

Second, the Federal Fair Housing Act of 1968, has diminished overt racial discrimination in housing markets, though real estate a-gents and mortgage lending policies of banks have continued in less overt ways to direct black households seeking suburban housing to particular suburban areas.[4] Nevertheless, the overall climate of racial attitudes has probably improved making whites more receptive to black neighbors and blacks more comfortable in seeking suburban housing.[5,6] Housing discrimination, however, remains pervasive in both rental and purchase markets according to a recent study under-taken for the U.S. Department of Housing and Urban Development.[7]

Exclusionary Barriers

Rising black prosperity coupled with explicit government sanctions against discrimination in constructing, purchasing, and renting dwellings has undoubtedly been the major impetus for the movement to suburbs of middle and upper income black households. Those who are less prosperous, even including households at the lower end of the middle income spectrum, have found the suburbs less hospitable. Many suburban communities, supported by a longstanding judicial bias in favor of the validity of municipal land-use regulations, have adopted no-growth, limited growth, and biased growth land-use controls. These controls influence not only the availability of land for residential development, but also the price of land and therefore the cost of residential development.[8] Land parcels of any use-class and size will tend to rise in price as their supply is restricted through zoning.[9] In addition, by setting low ceilings on residential densities, suburban communities can make the cost of higher density, low and moderate income development so high that private developers will turn to more profitable pursuits. Municipal housing authorities who, like private developers are eligible for "Section 8" federal housing development assistance, may find it difficult to support this type of development.[10]

There are still other ways for suburban communities to frustrate the provision of low and moderate income housing. Minimum house size requirements, extensive and costly subdivision requirements, administrative delays, and expensive though arbitrary demands in exchange for local building permits further inflate the costs of residential construction.[11] The existence of these conditions, is not necessarily an indication of exclusionary intent, of course. Suburban municipalities also constrain low and moderate income housing development by restricting annual utility hook-ups, levying special assessments on remote parcels to cover site improvements, and limiting investment in capital facilities necessary to support new housing and new residents. New Jersey is a case in point. This State imposes budget "caps" on annual rates of increase in government spending. Its municipalities may increase their budgets by no more than five percent per year, while school districts are restricted to an annual expenditure increment which is approximately equal to three-quarters of the annual increase in real estate value. Other states have recently passed referenda instituting limits on property tax rates which have a similar though not identical effect.[12] These limits on municipal spending, however, are certainly not on their face discriminatory. They do, however, limit the capacity of suburban communities to house additional residents, including blacks, and particularly the poor.

Institutional Response to Exclusionary Practices

Opposition to exclusionary land development practices has been pursued by government on several fronts. "Fair housing" legislation has ensured that black renters and buyers will not have to confront the more blatant, organized forms of discrimination in securing access to *existing* suburban housing. But still other government measures have been required to overcome the exclusionary land development practices which on their face simply restrict the production of low and moderate income suburban housing, but which, in reality, deny a large portion of the black community access to suburbs. These restrictive policies are especially inimical in the newer, mainly outer-ring suburbs that lack any older housing stock that might filter down to less wealthy households.[13]

A number of important steps to overcome the effects of exclusionary suburban development regulations have been taken through litigation. Probably the most prominent and far-reaching decision was that, not of the United States Supreme Court, but of the Supreme Court of New Jersey. In March, 1975, this court struck down restrictive zoning laws of suburban Mount Laurel because they were determined to be economically discriminatory and therefore in violation of the state constitution's "general welfare" provisions.[14] Subsequently, the United States Supreme Court refused to hear Mount Laurel's appeal though it has generally refused to recognize "economic" discrimination except in voting and criminal cases. In subsequent litigation in the state, the courts now have begun to make more specific the criteria by which communities are to determine the amount of land and the number of low and moderate income dwelling units that constitute their "fair share" of the regional housing burden.[15] Still to be determined is how far such "developing" communities must go to demonstrate good faith.[16] Since the Mount Laurel decision similar suits have been filed in a number of other states.[17]

While the federal courts have tended not to be willing to question the motivations behind municipal zoning practices, their impact has been felt in other areas of litigation. In April, 1976, the United States Supreme Court determined that the federal judiciary has the authority to order the Department of Housing and Urban Development to promote subsidized public housing in suburbs when it can be demonstrated that it has previously promoted segregated housing by locating federally subsidized housing in predominantly black city neighborhoods.[18]

In addition, the courts have played a very active role in assessing and directing efforts to afford blacks greater access to educational institutions and jobs. In the important Bakke decision, of June, 1978, the United States Supreme Court ruled that while the rigid minority quota system for medical school admissions at the University of California at Davis was unacceptable, affirmative action programs could be justified by a variety of other factors, among which is the existence of past discrimination which such programs could properly remedy.[19] Similar litigation regarding affirmative action employment practices is currently before the courts.

The major federal enforcement agencies now promote voluntary compliance with the prescriptions against employment discrimination found in Title VII of the Civil Rights Act of 1964 and Executive Order 11246 pertaining to employers having federal contracts. The Supreme Court will soon hear a major case involving one voluntary program for minority hiring. In this case two lower federal courts have ruled that Kaiser Aluminum's minority hiring plan was illegal. At issue is the intent of the 1964 Civil Rights Act regarding reverse racial discrimination in hiring programs when there is a record of previous discrimination.[20]

Federal legislation and subsequent court review, elaboration and extension have had, it seems, a significant impact on black education, earnings, and, therefore, access to suburban housing. To the extent that rising incomes have played a major role in recent black suburbanization, these seminal programs of affirmative action have made a substantial contribution.[21] In addition voluntary affirmative action hiring programs of suburban employers have surely given further impetus to the movement of blacks to suburbs.

Resolving Propulsive and Exclusionary Forces

The rate and character of black suburbanization is a product of the resolution of both propulsive forces and exclusionary practices. The propulsive include rising black income, the deterioration of non-suburban residential areas, and the massive development of new employment opportunities in and adjacent to suburban areas. Exclusionary practices are diverse and those which restrict suburban entry through the inflation of residential costs are not necessarily racially motivated. Indeed some would assert that only those suburban practices which explicitly exclude on the basis of race are truly exclusionary. Legal redress in these situations has already been secured in many instances, though in some situations there is yet surely cause for concern. That there remains a residue of explicitly racially motivated exclusionary practices can only be explained by examining the pervasiveness of the particular practice, the legal requirements of proof and standing to sue, and the degree to which the practice may be concealed from view.

Among suburban jurisdictions within single metropolitan areas, the balance of propulsive and exclusionary forces may differ considerably. Some communities therefore may be far more likely than others to experience increase in black population. If such imbalance is sustained over a long period of time, and if there is a substantial pool of black households seeking to reside in the suburbs, then the more "open" communities may become suburban ghettos. This may occur whether or not "white flight", that is, the accelerated departure of white households for racial reasons, occurs. Even in the absence of white flight, if there are only a few suburbs in which black households (for reasons of race or wealth) can reasonably expect to find dwellings, then racial transition may occur if there are more black than white households seeking available homes. They key point is that the probability of racial transition in single communities is influenced by the degree to which other suburban communities are open to blacks seeking dwellings.

In overview, we conclude that if a suburban community as a whole is inclined to exclude blacks and other minorities, the strategy it may choose to pursue will depend on a number of factors. These include the size and income distribution of the pool of black households potentially interested in residing in the suburbs, the number, size, and variety of alternate suburban residential areas, and the degree to which the income-exclusiveness of the suburban jurisdiction itself will effectively deny access to this particular pool of black households seeking suburban entry. Suburbs that have the intent of racial exclusion but are not income-exclusive may substitute more overt forms of racial exclusion.

Suburbs, of course, are not always internally of one mind. And the larger the community, the more diverse may be the racial attitudes within it. When, however, this diversity is submerged within an overall political consensus to take centralized, exclusionary governmental actions, then the exclusion may be complete. Not all exclusionary practices, in any case, are governmental. Lacking a central governmental mechanism to exclude, a community may find it more difficult to speak with one exclusionary voice.

Rationale for Policy-Intervention

Ultimately, there are several distinct reasons which might justify policy-intervention in the suburban residential process. The *first* concerns the existence of practices motivated by an explicit intent to exclude on the basis of race. Here, the precedent for governmental action is most firmly established. A *second* reason is exclusion on the basis of income. In this second instance the precedent for government intervention is less substantial. But when large segments of the population have been systematically excluded over many generations from the processes which generate and distribute wealth, then it can be argued that remedial action is appropriate. A *third* reason would be that impoverished blacks can realize a substantial benefit through residence in superior suburban environments.

Of these three reasons justifying policy-intervention in the suburban residential process, the first appeals to fundamental constitutional guarantees regarding the rights and duties of individuals in American society. The second reason acknowledges the cumulative effects of the interlocking consequences of limited access to jobs and residences. This reason might stand on its own, though it can be supported by the third which concerns the benefits which accrue to residents of quality suburban communities. Indeed, explicitly "racial" exclusionary practices have undoubtedly contributed to the quality of some suburban communities since through these practices they have avoided both the financial burden and the physical presence of poverty.

Historically, separate black residential environs have been "unequal". This inequality has been manifested in two distinct dimensions of difference. First, blacks have been less well served by their residential situations than *comparable* whites by theirs. Second, there has long existed a substantial difference between blacks and whites regarding their distribution among neighborhoods of varying quality. Today, given limited evidence of selective income-convergence between black and white, it might be asserted by some that residential equality in this second, more important sense is now a possibility. In fact, it might be possible to envision the existence of quality segregated black and white suburban communities, perhaps generated out of mutual preferences of blacks and whites for separate living spaces. It seems unlikely, however, that equality could be sustained in this situation, and further, mutual understanding would be far harder to foster. Clearly, the nebulous entanglements of the "separate but equal" syndrome take on new meanings in an era of improving conditions for many but hardly all blacks.

NOTES

1. For an examination of the impact of the "war on poverty" initiated in the 1960's see Robert Haveman, "Poverty, Income Distribution and Social Policy: The Last Decade and the Next," Discussion Paper No. 365-76 (Madison University of Wiscosnin, Institute for Research on Poverty, 1976). See also, Robert Plotnik and Felicity Skidmore, *Progress Against Poverty: A Review of the 1964-74 Decade* (New York: Academic Press, 1975).

2. Between 1965 and 1977, the number of black college students increased from 274,000 to 1.1 million. About 11 percent of all college students today are black. Diane Ravitch, "60's Education, 70's Benefits," *New York Times*, June 29, 1978. But see Christopher Jencks *et al.*, *Inequality: A Reassessment of the Effect of Family and Schooling in America* (New York: Basic Books, 1972).

3. James P. Smith and Finis R. Welch, "Race Differences in Earnings: A Survey and New Evidence," R-2295-NSF (Santa Monica, California: RAND Corporation, 1978). But see also, S.H. Masters, *Black-White Income Differentials: Empirical Studies and Policy Implications* (New York: Academic Press, Research on Poverty Monograph Series, 1975). Not all, of course, will agree either that significant black progress has occurred or that the rate of black-white income convergence has been as rapid as it should have been. See, for example, Robert B. Hill, "The Illusion of Black Progress," *Social Policy*, (November/December 1978), 14-25. Hill stresses the continuing disparity not only between blacks and whites, but also between the black middle class and less prosperous blacks.

4. All the more blatant types of racial discrimination are now prohibited in renting and selling dwellings which have been developed with any form of government assistance. In addition, racial discrimination is also prohibited in purchase and rental assistance through direct subsidies, mortgage assistance and the like. But while racial discrimination is illegal, "economic" discrimination is not.

   It now appear that the American real estate industry is undergoing a massive transformation. Some estimate that in the near future perhaps just ten large real estate firms will dominate the single family home market. Exactly how this centralization of sales networks will influence future central city and suburban racial patterns is not yet clear. Peter T. Kilborn, "Corporate Giants Invade the Residential Market," *New York Times*, February 4, 1979.

5. There is substantial evidence of racial "steering" by realtors in major metropolitan areas across the country. See Risa Palm, *Urban Social Geography from the Perspective of the Real Estate Salesman* (Berkeley:

Center for Real Estate and Urban Economics, University of California, Research Report No. 38, 1976), and also Risa Palm, "Spatial Segmentation of the Urban Housing Market," *Economic Geography*, Vo. 54, No. 3 (July 1978), 210-221. And, for evidence of price effects see J.F. Kain and J.M. Quigley, *Housing Markets and Racial Discrimination: A Microeconomic Analysis* (New York: National Bureau of Economic Research, 1975), as well as A.B. Schnare and R.J. Struyk, "Segmentation in Urban Housing Markets," *Journal of Urban Economics*, Vol. 3 (1976), 146-66, and B.J.L. Berry and R.S. Bednarz, "A Hedonic Model of Prices and Assessments for Single-Family Homes: Does the Assessment Follow the Market or the Market Follow the Assessment?", *Land Economics* Vol. 51 (1975), 21-40.

6. While the Federal Fair Housing Act of 1968 helped open the way for blacks seeking suburban residences directly, it also stimulated the passage of "open housing" laws in many suburban communities across the country. In many communities these have insured at least token black representation. But some communities have experienced substantial black increase due to at least two factors: the desire of some blacks to live in places where there is a significant black population, and "racial steering" by realtors seeking not to offend some predominantly white communities in order to preserve access to those real estate markets.

Some communities to which blacks have been directed now seem destined to be "resegregated" as suburban ghettos. Such communities, seeking to halt the succession process and preserve their integrated identity have enacted open housing laws to insure that realtors would have to inform whites of housing opportunities in the area while directing blacks elsewhere. A case in point is Bellwood, a Chicago suburb, which requires all home-sellers to inform city hall of their intent to sell. It also requires town approval for brokers to solicit listings and operates a public relations bureau to monitor sales and publicize the multi-racial character of the community. It sued several brokers for racial steering in violation of the U.S. Fair Housing Act of 1968. Now the town's standing to sue in racial steering cases has been confirmed by the Supreme Court, even as realtors, *allied with some blacks who claim they are being denied access to suburbs with significant minority populations*, are mounting a strong new legal offensive against "integration-maintenance" plans. The outcome will have national significance. At issue is freedom of individuals to live where they please, versus the desire of society to achieve social purposes that are believed to relate to the racial mix of suburbs.

Despite the role of the U.S. Civil Rights Act of 1968 in the Bellwood and other similar cases, there is today substantial evidence that the Act has not been particulary effective in banning discrimination in the sale and rental of housing. This is because under the 1968 law persons who believe they have suffered discrimination have just two options. One is to bear the costs of lawsuits which may take years to resolve. The other is to appeal to the U.S. Department of Housing and Urban Development whose role is restricted to mediation between the prospective occupant and the landlord or seller. This Department, however, does not have the authority to enforce remedies and therefore is an ineffective participant in the process. Currently under consideration in both houses of Congress is a bill—the Fair Housing Amendments of 1979—which would extend the scope of the anti-bias mandate while empowering the Department with the authority to grant temporary injunctive relief while cases are pending, and punish violators, with the assistance of the Justice Department. Real estate interests are strongly opposed to this legislation and it is probably unlikely the bill would become law in its present form.

7. This study, undertaken by the National Committee against Discrimination in Housing, Inc., examines housing markets in forty cities across the country. Black and white auditors would visit residential units in succession. On average, discrimination was encountered at one in four rental units, and in addition, two of three blacks seeking to purchase units experienced some measure of discrimination. Preliminary findings are reported in Frederick J. Eggers, *et al.*, "Background Information and Initial Findings of the Housing Market Practices Survey" (Washington, D.C.: U.S. Department of Housing and Urban Development, April 17, 1978).

8. A number of municipalities have recently instituted no-growth and limited growth regulations. Petaluma, California has successfully defended its plan to limit annual residential building permits in court. See Earl Finkler *et al.*, *Urban Nongrowth* (New York: Praeger, 1976). See also, James W. Hughes, "Dilemmas of Suburbanization and Growth Controls," *Annals of the American Academy of Political and Social Science*, (1975), 422, 61-76..

9. In the New York metropolitan area almost 100 percent of all undeveloped land zoned for residential purposes is devoted to single-family housing. More than half of all residential-zoned vacant land in Connecticut is limited to one and two acre lots.

10. See also, L.S. Rubinowitz, *Low-Income Housing: Suburban Strategies* (Cambridge, Massachusetts: Ballinger, 1974), and C.M. Haar and D.S. Iatridis, *Housing the Poor in Suburbia: Public Policy at the Grass Roots* (Cambridge, Massachusetts: Ballinger, 1974).

11. These exclusionary policies are reviewed in considerable detail in a recent report of the American Bar Association's Advisory Commission on Housing and Urban Growth. Richard P. Fishman (ed.), *Housing For All Under Law: New Directions in Housing, Land Use and Planning Law—A Report of the American Bar Association's Advisory Commission on Housing and Urban Growth* (Cambridge, Massachusetts: Ballinger, 1978). See also, Donald Foley, "Institutional and Contextual Factors Affecting the Housing Choices of Minority Residents," in *Segregation in Residential Areas*, edited by Amos H. Hawley and Vincent P. Rock (Washington, D.C.: National Academy of Sciences, 1973), reprinted in *The Manipulated City: Perspectives on Spatial Structure and Social Issues in Urban America*, edited by S. Gale and E.G. Moore (Chicago: Maaroufa Press, 1975), 168-181; and E.M. Bergman, *Eliminating Exclusionary Zoning: Reconciling Workplace and Residence in Suburban Areas* (Cambridge, Massachusetts: Ballinger, 1974).

12. In 1978, California voters passed "Proposition 13" limiting property taxes to 1.5 percent of property values. In all, thirteen states voted on tax or spending referenda in 1978 with varied results. Some states, such as New York, already have constitutional limitations on property tax rates. As the cost of labor, materials and money has risen at a steady rate of six or seven percent per annum in the last several years, the slack in capped

budgets has diminished making communities more prone to maintain existing activities than to seek to expand through development of vacant lands. Of course, some fiscal limits are tied to the total pooled value of property. In such cases the budget limit will rise with growth through new development.

13. Clearly one of the major dynamics of racial succession in older residential areas is through the filtering of residential units from one occupant group to another, often less prosperous group. Since in many areas blacks are proportionally more numerous in the lower income strata, the process of filtering will often create the opportunity for both income and racial succession to occur. See Wallace F. Smith, *Filtering and Neighborhood Change*, Research Report No. 24 (Berkeley: The University of California, the Center for Real Estate and Urban Economics, Institute of Urban and Regional Development, 1964); and John B. Lansing, Charles W. Clifton and James N. Morgan, *New Homes and Poor People: A Study of Chain Moves* (Ann Arbor, Michigan: University of Michigan, Institute for Social Research, 1969).

14. In its Mount Laurel decision the New Jersey Supreme Court said suburban areas "must permit multi-family housing, without bedroom or similar restrictions, as well as small dwellings on very small lots, low-cost housing of other types and, in general, high density zoning, without artificial and unjustifiable minimum requirements as to lot size, building site and the like, to meet the full panoply of . . . needs. . . for all categories of people who may desire to live there.[33] *Southern Burlington County NAACP v. Mount Laurel*, 67 N.J. 191, 336 A.2d 713 (1975). See also Jerome G. Rose, *After Mount Laurel: The New Suburban Zoning* (New Brunswick: Rutgers University, Center for Urban Policy Research, 1977). See also, David Listokin, *Fair Share Housing Allocation* (New Brunswick: Rutgers University, Center for Urban Policy Research, 1976).

15. Recently the New Jersey Supreme Court has held that zoning ordances which are prima facie exclusionary, regardless of intent, may justify zoning revisions. *Oakwood at Madison, Inc. v. Township of Madison, N.J.*, A.2d, (Dkt no. A-80/81, 1977). The United States Supreme Court, however, has said in the Arlington Heights decision that intent to racially discriminate must be proven.

16. Since many New Jersey communities have already reached their state mandated budget caps, it is not yet clear whether they could accommodate additional low- and moderate-income residents without exceeding these spending limits. Still, good faith may require a more positive response than simply zoning additional land for this type of housing.

17. See also Kenneth Pearlman, "The Closing Door: The Supreme Court and Residential Segregation," *Journal of the American Institute of Planners*, Vol. 44, No. 2 (April 1978), 160-69, which considers both constitutional and statutory remedies for suburban exclusion.

18. As a result of this, the Gautreaux decision, the federal courts have decreed that no more public housing and only limited amounts of subsidized, Section 8 private housing can be provided in black areas until more is provided in the suburban counties around Chicago. See *Hills v. Gautreaux*, 425 U.S. 284 (1976).

19. See *Bakke v. Regents of the University of California*, 553 U.S. 1152 (1976).

20. On December 12, 1978, the United States Supreme Court agreed to hear this case, *United Steelworkers v. Weber* (No. 78-432). This promises to be of major significance. In one recent study, however, it was concluded that government affirmative action programs have had little to do with the narrowing of the black-white wage gap. James P. Smith and Finis R. Welch, "Race Differences in Earnings: A Survey and New Evidence," R-2295-NSF (Santa Monica, California: RAND Corporation, 1978).

21. Some, however, assert that despite incontrovertible evidence of prior discrimination, programs of affirmative action may pose a challenge to individual freedom and identity which could outweigh the social benefits they pursue. Value conflicts may indeed be heightened in periods of deliberate social change, in fact they may sustain the process through the contraditions they embody. But see Nathan Glazer, *Affirmative Discrimination: Ethnic Inequality and Public Policy* (New York: Basic Books, 1975), and Barry R. Gross, *Discrimination in Reverse: Is Turnabout Fair Play?* (New York: New York University Press, 1978). See also, D.A. Bell, "Affirmative Discrimination:Ethnic Inequality and Public Policy—A Review of Glazer," *Emory Law Journal*, Vol. 25 (February 1976).

3

Black Suburbanization in the Seventies

Fifty-five percent of the American black population still lives in central cities, and less than 20 percent lives in suburbs.[1] Further, not all those residing in central cities are impoverished nor are all who reside in suburbs either prosperous or ensconced in prosperous, life-enhancing neighborhoods.[2] It is commonly held nevertheless, that black suburbanization is desirable because it indicates rising black affluence, or growing interracial accord, or new hope for the black poor, or evidence of population dispersal as a prelude to central city revitalization. There are clearly many kinds of black suburbanization, differentiated by the identity, geographic origin, and suburban destination of black migrants.

Hard evidence regarding the scale, pace, substance, and geography of black suburbanization has been in short supply until recently. Therefore, it has been almost impossible to assess the effectiveness of various policies designed to open suburban housing markets to blacks or to determine the secondary consequences of black suburbanization for the suburbs themselves or for the places from which these suburban blacks have departed. Now this evidence is at hand and can be examined.

Major Information Sources

There are three major sources of information documenting black
suburbanization. One of these, of course, is the national decennial
census. This census has been prone to undercount blacks and other
sources must be used to measure change in intercensal years. Another
source is the Bureau of the Census's monthly surveys reported in
several series of *Current Population Reports.* While only some
decennial census items are determined through sampling and therefore subject to sampling error, most information in these population
reports is based on samples of varying sizes. A third, and not yet
fully exploited source for both housing and resident population
characteristics is the Annual Housing Survey performed by the
United States Bureau of the Census for the Department of Housing
and Urban Development.[3] Since 1973, the Annual Housing Survey
has documented national housing conditions using three distinct
samples.[4] This survey is helpful in documenting both dwelling unit
and household characteristics of blacks living in suburbs and com-
paring these households with their white suburban counterparts
and with the black population living in central cities. While the
national sample covers about 130 SMSA's, the users' computer
tapes suppress the geographic code identifying central city/non-
central city location in all but 50 SMSA's, most of which also are
included in the annual rotating samples of the nation's major SMSA's.
Annual Housing Survey data included in this and later chapters
are derived, as indicated, from published reports as well as from
direct analysis using the Survey's national sample users' tape since
much survey information cannot be retrieved from the published
summary tables. Of course, not all survey results are included on
these tapes. This study relies on the annual national survey tape
rather than the SMSA survey tapes because it affords more extensive SMSA coverage in any one year. Examination of individual
SMSA's, however, requires the use of the SMSA surveys since their
sampling rates are far higher and their results more reliable.

Each of these major data sources employs the concept of the
Census Bureau's Standard Metropolitan Statistical Area. This area
contains either one central city of at least 50,000 people, or two
central cities whose joint population is 50,000 or more with the
population of the smaller of the two 15,000. The SMSA, more
precisely, is a set of contiguous counties containing the county or
counties in which the central city resides plus outlying counties
interacting with the central city.[5] Over time the boundaries of the
central city may change through annexation or consolidation, and

additional counties may meet the criteria for SMSA inclusion. In addition, new urban places may rise to SMSA status. For these reasons suburbanization data must be interpreted cautiously. Data from the Annual Housing Survey, however, pertain only to the 243 SMSA's used in the 1970 census.[6] Changes in SMSA definition criteria, boundaries, and titles made after February, 1971, are not reflected in Survey tabulations.

Generally, the concepts and definitions of the Annual Housing Survey and the 1970 Census are comparable though the Survey also includes items not appearing in the Census. The Current Population Reports of the Current Population Survey that covers household and family characteristics, population mobility and income, however, may contain information which is not wholly consistent with the Annual Housing Survey due to sampling variability, survey technique and processing procedures. The primary concepts and definitions are essentially the same in both surveys, except in relation to income.

Some Basic Definitions

To examine Black suburbanization some basic definitions are needed. Given the major sources of recent national urban demographic information, "suburbs" must be defined as the non-central city portions of Standard Metropolitan Statistical Areas. Racial identification does not denote the application of precise scientific definitions of biological stock. Rather, the decennial census used a self-classification procedure while the Annual Housing Survey distinguishes White, Black and Other according to enumerator judgment. Black households are usually defined to be those whose "head" is black, regardless of composition.

Current Perspectives on the Racial Geography of Metropolitan Areas

The national residential pattern of the black population is the culmination of pervasive forces not wholly shared with the population at large. There persist black-white geographic differentials attesting not only to the unique geographic history of the black population, but also to the special conditions of resources, preferences and residential opportunity that now govern the changing geography of black residence.

In 1977, 4.6 million blacks, or 18.8 percent of the national black population, resided in the non-central city, "suburban" portion of metropolitan areas.[7] At the same time 13.5 million, or 55.0 percent lived in central cities, while 6.4 million or 26.2 percent lived in non-metropolitan areas. In contrast, 77.2 million or 41.9 percent of the national white population resided in suburban areas, while 45.0 million (24.4 percent) lived in central cities, and 62.2 million (33.7 percent) were in nonmetropolitan areas. Blacks were consequently vastly underrepresented in suburban areas, overrepresented in central cities and somewhat less than proportionately present in nonmetropolitan areas (Exhibit 1).

Between 1960 and 1977, the national black population increased by 6.1 million (33.4 percent), far out-pacing the remainder of the population which increased by 28.0 million (17.9 percent).[8] But, while the number of suburban blacks increased in these years by 1.9 million (71.8 percent), the proportion of all blacks who resided in suburbs increased from 14.6 percent in 1960 to just 18.8 percent in 1977.[9] *Thus, while there indeed have occurred substantial percentage increases in the number of blacks residing in suburbs since 1960, the initial base was very small, and consequently, the percentage of all blacks residing in suburbs has increased almost imperceptibly (Exhibit 1).*

National Shifts and the Reemergence of Nonmetropolitan Areas

Black suburbanization, it must be stressed, is not an isolated process, detached from trends within black and white populations at large. Suburban gains must have their counterparts in relative non-suburban losses. They measure the differential and the unique appeal of suburbs over other residential locales. From 1960 to 1970, the average annual (compounded) rate of black increase in metropolitan areas (2.87 percent) stood in striking contrast to the average annual loss rate of the nonmetropolitan black component (−0.55 percent). In these years moreover, central city (2.97 percent) and suburban (2.53 percent) annual increase rates were nearly the same (Exhibit 1).

Since 1970, however, there has begun a remarkable shift. From 1970 to 1974, the overall annual (compounded) rate of black increase in metropolitan areas fell to just 2.27 percent, while the long-standing decline of the nonmetropolitan black population was reversed as the annual rate of nonmetropolitan increase rose to 0.15 percent per year. These trends were drastically accelerated in the ensuing three years. From 1974 to 1977, the annual rate of metropolitan black increase fell to just 0.32 percent per year while the rate of nonmetropolitan black increase rose precipitously to 3.79 percent per year.

EXHIBIT 1

POPULATION CHANGE BY RACE AND METROPOLITAN STATUS, 1960 TO 1977

	Metropolitan Area[1]			
	Total	*Inside Central Cities*[2]	*Outside Central Cities (Suburbs)*	*Nonmetropolitan*
A. *Population (thousands)*				
Black				
1960	12,311	9,636	2,675	6,037
1970	16,342	12,909	3,433	5,714
1977	18,048	13,451	4,596	6,427
White				
1960	104,176	48,845	55,331	52,182
1970	118,938	48,909	70,029	56,338
1977	122,177	44,951	77,226	62,158
B. *Percent Change*[3]				
Black				
1960-70	32.7(2.87)	34.0(2.97)	28.3(2.53)	-5.4(-0.55)
1970-74	9.4(2.27)	6.7(1.64)	19.5(4.55)	0.6(0.15)
1974-77	1.0(0.32)	-2.4(-0.79)	12.1(3.87)	11.8(3.79)
White				
1960-70	14.2(1.33)	0.1(0.01)	26.6(2.38)	7.8(0.77)
1970-74	2.5(0.61)	-4.4(-1.12)	7.3(1.77)	5.8(1.43)
1974-77	0.2(0.08)	-3.9(-1.31)	2.8(0.93)	4.2(1.39)

Notes: 1. Standard Metropolitan Statistical Areas are defined by their 1970 boundaries.
           2. Central City data for 1974 exclude annexations since 1970.
           3. Numbers in parentheses are average (compounded) annual rates of change.

Source: U.S. Bureau of the Census, *Current Population Reports,* Series p-23, Nos. 37, 55 and 75, "Social and Economic Characteristics of the Metropolitan and Non-metropolitan Population," (Washington, D.C.: U.S. Government Printing Office, 1971, 1975 and 1978).

This latter figure was the net result of slowing rates of nonmetropolitan out-migration, natural increase and the highly selective
movement of blacks from metropolitan areas both to nearby nonmetropolitan areas and to more distant regions.[10]

But while these shifts in metropolitan and nonmetropolitan rates
of change are significant, a far more dramatic transition has occurred
within metropolitan areas. First, the average annual rate of central
city black increase has fallen from 2.97 percent during 1960-70, to
1.64 percent in the period from 1970 to 1974 and subsequently, to
an annual *loss* rate of −0.79 during 1974-77. Suburban rates of
increase have varied more irregularly in recent years. The average
annual rate of black suburban increase rose from 2.53 percent
during 1960-70, to 4.55 percent during 1970-74, and most recently
it has fallen to just 3.87 percent between 1974 and 1977. The
emerging picture is one of absolute annual black decline in central
cities, primarily due to accelerating rates of net out-migration from
the largest central cities, while both suburban areas and nonmetropolitan areas experience comparably high rates of black increase.

Zero Metropolitan Population Growth

Since 1960, black and white trends have generally been similar
in direction but not degree (Exhibit 1).[11] Average annual rates of
metropolitan increase have steadily fallen since 1960 for both
groups, though the slowing of black rates has been more pronounced.
Likewise, annual rates of nonmetropolitan increase have risen significantly for both, though the black rate has accelerated faster. Within
metropolitan areas the scene is more complex. Both groups have
experienced the advance from positive to negative rates of annual
central city change in the aggregate since 1960, but there is considerable variation among cities of varying sizes. Generally, in recent
years the larger cities have experienced the most drastic net annual
losses.[12]

Suburbs are unique among these geographical categories since the
black and white rates of annual change have evolved since 1960 in
different directions. Average annual rates of white suburban increase
have steadily fallen since 1960, while black rates have risen, and at
a rate far exceeding the rate of deceleration in the annual rate of
white suburban increase. In summary, both racial groups have moved
toward zero metropolitan population growth, while the annual rate
of black nonmetropolitan growth exceeds the white by a factor of
almost three. Whites are fleeing central cities in the aggregate somewhat more rapidly than blacks, while in the suburbs, the black population is increasing four times as rapidly as the white.

By 1977, 5.7 million more blacks lived in metropolitan areas than did so in 1960, while just 0.4 million lived in nonmetropolitan areas. Simultaneously there was a gain of 1.9 million in suburbs. In these same years the white metropolitan population rose by 18.0 million and the nonmetropolitan population by 10.0 million. The white central city population declined by 3.9 million as the suburbs increased by almost 21.9 million. Thus most of the increase in white population since 1960, eighty percent, resides in suburbs, while most of the black increase, over sixty percent, resides in central cities. And during the period from 1960 to 1977, 8.4 percent or about one in twelve new suburban residents is black. From 1970 to 1977 though, over 13.9 percent or about one in seven new suburban residents is black.

Black Concentration and Racial Shift in Metropolitan Areas

Blacks constituted 11.5 percent of the national population in 1977, up from 10.6 percent in 1960. In 1977, they were proportionately represented in metropolitan areas (12.6 percent of the total population), but were considerably overrepresented in central cities (22.4 percent) generally, and especially in central cities associated with metropolitan areas exceeding one million population (27.8 percent) (Exhibit 2). They constituted 16.3 percent of the population in central cities of metropolitan areas having fewer than one million persons, between five and six percent of suburban populations regardless of the size of the metropolitan area, and 9.3 percent of the nonmetropolitan population, in the same year.

Over time the racial proporations have fluctuated due to changes in both black and total population. Since 1960, these proportions have varied only slightly, and somewhat irregularly, in the areas in which blacks are least well represented, namely suburbs and nonmetropolitan areas. In the areas where they are overrepresented however, these proportions have steadily increased. It is particularly noteworthy that, on the whole, the degree to which blacks are overrepresented has increased most rapidly in the larger central cities where they have for some time been present in disproportionate numbers (Exhibit 2). As a general rule, the larger the initial proportion black, the higher the rate at which this proportion has increased.[13]

Summary

Dramatic changes in the growth regimen of urban America have occurred in the last two decades. These changes, some of which were

EXHIBIT 2 BLACK POPULATION AS PERCENT OF TOTAL, BY SIZE OF METROPOLITAN AREA: 1960, 1970 AND 1977			
Location of Residence	*1960*	*1970*	*1977*
UNITED STATES	10.6	11.1	11.5
Metropolitan Areas[1]	10.7	11.9	12.6
Central Cities	16.4	20.5	22.4
Central Cities in Metropolitan Areas:			
1,000,000 or more	18.8	25.2	27.8
Less than 1,000,000	13.2	14.9	16.3
Suburbs	4.8	4.6	5.5
Suburbs in Metropolitan Areas:			
1,000,000 or more	4.0	4.5	5.9
Less than 1,000,000	5.9	4.8	5.0
Nonmetropolitan Areas	10.3	9.1	9.3

Note: 1. Excludes Middlesex and Somerset Counties in New Jersey. Metropolitan areas pertain to the number, size, and boundaries of 1970.

Source: U.S. Bureau of the Census, *Current Population Reports*, Special Studies, Series P-23, No. 54, "The Social and Economic Status of the Black Population in the United States, 1974," Table 6, and Series P-23, No. 75, "Social and Economic Characteristics of the Metropolitan and Nonmetropolitan Population: 1977 and 1970," Table 3.

not wholly apparent even as late as the last national census, have been shared by black and white alike. But the degree to which black and white have experienced these changes has been significantly different. Since 1960, the annual rate of increase in the growth of the metropolitan population has diminished substantially. This has been a product of the selective abandonment of the central city by both blacks and whites, coupled with a marginal increase in the aggregate population of the suburban realm. In these same years, nonmetropolitan areas, particularly those nearby the nation's major metropolitan centers, have begun to win an increasing share of new population growth.

Rates of change in cities, suburbs and beyond, of course, would differ between blacks and whites even if there were no migration among theses classes of places. This is because of two things. First, rates of natural increase vary among these places within racial categories. And second, the rate of natural increase in the black in the black population at large is substantially higher than for the white.

The most significant differences in rates of population change between blacks and whites pertain to the suburbs. From 1960 to 1970, the average annual rate of black suburban increase was 2.53 percent. And this rate has accelerated since then: 4.55 percent, 1970-74, and 3.87 percent during 1974-77. White rates of annual suburban increase were comparable to the black during the 1960's but fell precipitously after 1970, reflecting the overall downturn in their rate of aggregate natural increase. Both black and white rates of nonmetropolitan increase have likewise accelerated since 1960, with the rate of black increase being most pronounced.

The spatial reconfiguration of the black population is not an abstract process. Rather, it reflects and sustains a plethora of motivations, attitudes and frustrations. Black and white are interlinked in this process of change, responding to each other and to a common environment of geographic opportunities. The interaction, driven by the national economy, shaped by politics and policy, and moderated by evolving norms of racial accord, is a key dynamic in the social order of urban society.

NOTES

1. For an examination of the residential configuration of blacks in central cities see Annemette Sorenson, Karl E. Taeuber and Leslie J. Hollingsworth, Jr., "Indexes of Racial Residential Segregation for 109 Cities in the United States, 1940 to 1970," *Sociological Focus* (April 1975), 125-142; Ann B. Schnare, *Residential Segregation by Race in U.S. Metropolitan Areas: An Analysis Across Cities and Over Time* (Washington, D.C.: The Urban Institute, February 1977); and , of course, Karl E. Taeuber and Alma F. Taeuber, *Negroes in Cities: Residential Segregation and Neighborhood Change* (Chicago: Aldine Publishing Company, 1965). See also, Karl E. Taeuber, "Racial Segregation: The Persisting Dilemma," *Annals of the American Academy of Political and Social Science* (November 1975), 87-96.

2. See Bernard J. Frieden, "Blacks in Suburbia: The Myth of Better Opportunities," in *Minority Perspectives*, series editor, L. Wingo (Baltimore: Johns Hopkins University Press, for Resources for the Future, Inc., The Governance of Metropolitan Regions No. 2, 1972), pp. 31-49; P. Delaney, "Negroes Find Few Tangible Gains," in *Suburbia in Transition*, edited by L.H.Masotti and J.K.Hadden (New York: New Viewpoints for the New York Times, 1974), 278-82; Harold M. Rose, "The All-Black Town: Suburban Prototype or Rural Slum?" in *People and Politics in Urban Society*, edited by Harlan Haber (Beverly Hills, California: Sage Publications, Inc., 1972), 397-431; David Harvey, "Revolutionary and Counter-Revolutionary Theory in Geography, and the Problem of Ghetto Formation," in *Perspectives in Geography 2: The Geography of the Ghetto—Perceptions, Problems, and Alternatives*, edited by Harold M.Rose (DeKalb: Northern Illinois

University Press, 1972), 2-25; and David Harvey, "The Political Economy of Urbanization in the Advanced Capitalist Countries: The Case of the U.S.," in the *Urban Affairs Annual Review* (Beverly Hills, California: Sage Publications, 1975).

3. The survey is authorized by the Housing and Urban Development Act of 1970.

4. First, there is a national sample of 76,000 designated dwelling units of all types in all places, whether occupied or not. This sample of one in approximately ten units is repeated in successive years, with adjustments for demolitions, conversions and new construction. Second, the twelve largest SMSA's in 1973 were divided into three groups of four. Each year one group is examined in a three-year rotation using a sample size of 15,000 per SMSA. Equal numbers of sample units are taken from the central city and non-central city parts of each SMSA. Third, each year, also in a three-year rotation, about sixteen other SMSA's are examined using samples of 5,000. Both SMSA samples were initiated in 1974 while the national sample, which includes sample units in about 130 SMSA's was begun in 1973, though year-to-year unit tracking has been possible only since 1974. Only recently have the smaller-sample SMSA reports been disaggregated by central city and non-central city areas of SMSA's. Because these samples are quite small, they may not provide a good indication of black suburbanization.

5. New England SMSA's are formed by contiguous towns and cities, not counties.

6. These 243 include the 228 SMSA's identified in the Bureau of the Budget publication, *Standard Metropolitan Statistical Areas: 1967* (Washington, D.C.: Government Printing Office, 1967), plus fifteen SMSA's added before March, 1971, based on the results of the 1970 Census.

7. The pertinent boundaries are indicated in corresponding Exhibits. All time series data utilize constant 1970 boundaries unless otherwise indicated.

8. Most of this increase, of course, was due to natural increase, however, in these years there has also occurred a significant in-migration to the American mainland of blacks, most of whom came from the Carribbean. During 1971-75, it is estimated that 138,000 blacks came from there to New York State alone. Indeed, this may understate the number since many more may have arrived illegally. Eli Evans, "The City, South and Caribbean (II)," *New York Times*, June 27, 1978.

9. The relative contribution of migration and natural increase to change in black suburban population varies widely among the larger SMSA's. Larry H. Long, "How the Racial Composition of Cities Changes," *Land Economics*, Vol. LI, No. 3 (August 1975), 264.

10. Long distance migration historically has been an important ingredient in the pursuit of jobs and better conditions by blacks. See John Fraser Hart, "The Changing Distribution of the American Negro," *Annals, Association of American Geographers*, Vol. 50, No. 3 (September 1960), 242-66; T. Lynn Smith, "The Redistribution of the Negro Population of the United States, 1910-1960," *The Journal of Negro History*, Vol. LI, No. 3 (July 1966), 155-173); and also, Wesley C. Calef and Howard J. Nelson, "Distribution of Negro Population in the United States," *Geographical Review*,

Vol. 46, No. 1 (January 1956). For the last decade there has been a large flow of population to the South and West from the North. In this flow were many more prosperous black households whose individual paths were the reverse of the historical black pattern. But not until 1975 did the new southern prosperity induce much of a shift of poorer blacks from North to South while causing a slowing in the rate of the migration of poorer black households out of the South, according to Larry Long in the United States Bureau of the Census publication, "Interregional Migration of the Poor: Some Recent Changes," *Current Population Reports*, Series P-23, No. 73 (Washington, D.C.: Government Printing Office, 1978).

11. This paragraph examines black-white differences regarding the direction in which average annual rates of population change by geographical class (central city, suburb and nonmetropolitan area) have evolved from 1960 70, to 1970-74 and then to 1974-77. The rate of change of these annual change rates may either increase (accelerate) or decrease (decelerate). Since the black rate of natural increase was nearly twice the white rate during 1960-77, the overall degree of black population change by geographic class would tend to have a larger absolute numerical value than the white counterpart. It is in some ways more appropriate, therefore, to compare variations by race among geographic classes than to compare between races in single classes.

12. Data regarding demographic change among cities of different sizes have generally not been made available in intercensal years.

13. This relationship between initial proportion black and subsequent rate of increase in proportion Black held true, generally, from 1960 to 1970. Then as now the larger central cities had higher black proportions. Consequently, it would be expected that the larger the central city, the greater would be the numerical difference between the rates of black increase and white change. This is exactly what seems to have occurred. This difference for central cities in SMSA's exceeding two million was 50.1 percent. For those SMSA's having between one and two million it was 35.8 percent, and for those in SMSA's having between one-half to one million it was 22.3 percent. The difference for cities in SMSA's having one-quarter to one-half million was 17.1 percent, and for those in SMSA's under one-quarter million it was 10.0 percent. Comparable data are not available for intercensal years since 1970, but these trends have probably been sustained since 1970. The rule does not hold for suburbs during the last two decades. U.S.Bureau of the Census, *Census of Population and Housing, 1970*, U.S. Summary, Final Report, "General Demographic Trends for Metropolitan Areas, 1960 to 1970," Series PHC (2), (Washington, D.C.: U.S. Government Printing Office, 1971), Tables E and 9.

4

Interregional Differences in the Shape and Pace of Black Suburbanization

Aggregate national statistics tend to conceal significant inter-regional differences regarding racial composition and change in cities and suburbs. These differences issue from unique regional histories and their structural by-products in the form of social and economic relations within which the black community is positioned. The majority of black Americans trace, some through several generations, back to the American South, a region which still claims over half (53.7 percent, 1977) of the national black population.[1] The North-east (17.1 percent) and North Central (20.4 percent) states now hold 36.5 percent, while the West, a region distinguished by many dimensions of diversity, claims just 8.8 percent. This interregional distribution has held almost constant since 1960, despite a substantial exchange of migrants among regions.

Broad Dimensions of Differences

The configuration of the black demography is similar in both the Northeast and North Central states. In both about three-quarters of the black population lives in central cities, and about four in five of these live in the central cities associated with SMSA's having over one million population in 1977. In the Northeast 16.9 percent of all blacks live in the suburbs of SMSA's having over one million population, and just 3.3 percent live in the suburbs of the smaller SMSA's. In the North Central states, just 11.8 percent of all blacks live in the suburbs of SMSA's having in excess of one million persons, while 3.3 percent of all blacks living in the suburbs of the smaller SMSA's. The prototype of the northern smokestack city is home for one out of four American blacks.[2]

The West offers a distinct contrast. There 62.6 percent of all blacks live in central cities while 34.3 percent live in suburban locales. There also are the highest black suburban percentages of any of the major census regions. About 28.6 percent of all blacks residing in the West live in the suburbs of SMSA's having over one million persons, and 5.7 percent live in the suburbs of the SMSA's having fewer than one million persons in 1977. If the West is the most suburban of the major census regions, the South is the most "nonmetropolitan". There, fully 44.3 percent of the entire southern black population resides in nonmetropolitan areas and four in five of these reside in rural counties having no urban place over 25,000 population. Just 38.5 percent of the southern blacks reside in central cities, and of these, three in five are in cities whose SMSA's had fewer than one million persons in 1977. Only 8.0 percent of southern blacks reside in the suburbs of SMSA's having over one million population, and 9.2 percent reside in the suburbs of the SMSA's having fewer than one million in 1977. In sum, regarding blacks, the Northeast and North Central regions are the most "urban", the West, most "suburban", and the South, most "rural".

It is not surprising, given these interregional differences, that rates of black suburbanization differ substantially across regions (Exhibit 3). From 1970 to 1977, the nation's black suburban population increased by just over one-third (33.9 percent), within constant suburban boundaries delineated in 1970.[3,4] This rate was shared in the North Central (38.4 percent) and West (34.4 percent) regions.

In contrast, the Northeast recorded the slowest rate of increase, 12.6 percent, while the South had the greatest, 61.2 percent. Except in the West, there was an inverse relationship between the absolute number of suburban blacks in 1970 and the rate of black suburban increase. In the West, lower overall gross metropolitan densities plus lower aggregate black population and relatively low levels of absolute regional black increase may account for both the higher black suburban population in 1970, and the lower than expected rate of black suburban increase. Still, the absolute increase in the

EXHIBIT 3
BLACK POPULATION IN SUBURBS, BY REGION, 1977 AND 1970

(Numbers in thousands)

Region	Suburbs in all SMSA's				Suburbs in SMSA's over one million				Suburbs in SMSA's under one million			
	1977	1970	Change 1970-77 Absolute	Percent	1977	1970	Change 1970-77 Absolute	Percent	1977	1970	Change 1970-77 Absolute	Percent
Northeast	841	747	94	12.6	704	654	50	7.6	137	93	44	47.3
North Central	760	549	211	38.4	593	442	151	34.2	167	107	60	56.1
South	735	456	279	61.2	613	381	232	60.9	122	75	47	62.7
West	2260	1681	579	34.4	1046	573	473	82.5	1214	1108	106	9.6
U.S. Total	4596	3433	1163	33.9	2956	2050	906	44.2	1640	1383	257	18.6

Source: U.S. Census Bureau, *Current Population Reports*, Series P-23, No. 75, "Social and Economic Characteristics of Metropolitan and Nonmetropolitan Areas, 1977 and 1970" (Washington, D.C.: U.S. Government Printing Office, 1978), Table 3.

number of suburban blacks in the West was about equal to the total absolute increase in the three other regions *combined*.

Interregional Variations Summarized

At some risk of over-generalizing conditions in major census regions, it is possible to assemble brief characterizations of black suburbanization since 1970 in each. These follow.

> *Northeast*: This region realized the lowest absolute (94,000) and relative (12.6 percent) increases in the suburban black population of all the major regions. The increase was about equally divided between the suburbs of SMSA's exceeding one million total population and those having under one million, though the percent increase in the smaller SMSAs' suburbs was far higher than for the suburbs of the larger SMSA's (Exhibit 3).
> Several factors may explain the lower rates of black suburbanization in the Northeast. First, since 1970, there has occurred a substantial net regional black population loss due to net migration. From 1970 to 1977 this loss totaled 168,000 and since those leaving may have had higher income potential than those arriving, the result of net out-migration has been a reduced proportional capacity to suburbanize (Exhibit 4). The significance of migration for black suburbanization has apparently changed over time. Between 1965 and 1970, there was actually a net increase in the region's black population due to migration. In that period net migration increased the black population by 37,000, and in-migration was about 134 percent of out-migration. During the 1970's the annual net migration loss in black population has steadily increased, with the ratio of in- to out-migration rapidly falling. As this has occurred, the "mix" of in and out-migrators has probably changed. The average income of in-migrants may have fallen, but at the same time, not only may many more prosperous blacks be leaving the region but the number of low-income blacks who are annually departing also has probably increased due to the substantial job loss in the region's central cities as well as the reduction in central city spending on public services due to declining public revenues and increasing costs of service provision.
> A second major factor in the Northeast's low black suburbanization rate is the high and rapidly inflating cost of

EXHIBIT 4
NET MIGRATION FOR BLACK AND TOTAL POPULATION BY REGION,
1965-70, 1970-75 AND 1975-77

TIME PERIOD	In-Migration as a Percent of Out-Migration				NET MIGRATION[1] (Numbers in thousands)			
	Northeast	North Central	South	West	Northeast	North Central	South	West
1965-70								
TOTAL	64	76	126	143	−715	−637	656	696
BLACK	134	189	43	240	37	93	−217	87
1970-75								
TOTAL	44	59	181	143	−1,342	−1,195	1,829	708
BLACK	55	74	105	300	−64	−52	14	102
1975-77								
TOTAL	52	77	131	152	−615	−361	462	514
BLACK	29	115	110	404	−104	14	17	73

Notes: 1. Net migration is in-migration less out-migration.

Source: U.S. Bureau of the Census, *Census of Population: 1970*, Subject Reports, Final Report PG(2)-28, Mobility for States and Nations (Washington, D.C.: U.S. Government Printing Office, 1973); *Current Population Reports*, Series P-20, No. 320, February 1978, Table 42, and Series P-20, No. 285, October 1975, Table 30.

purchasing and renting dwellings in suburban areas. This reflects not only rising costs of inputs to residential construction, but also the amount of land, labor and capital needed to construct homes meeting minimum size and quality standards. The fact that rates of black suburbanization are so low in SMSA's having more than one million persons relative to rates in SMSA's under one million in the Northeast, may be due primarily to the higher cost and commensurately lower supply of suburban dwellings within the larger SMSA's.

Whatever the primary determinants of black suburbanization in the Northeast, relative to the racial composition of the region as a whole (8.6 percent black, 1977), blacks remain over-represented in central cities in SMSA's having more than one million population, about proportionately present in the central cities of SMSA's under one million and under-represented in suburbs and nonmetropolitan areas (Exhibit 5). Just 4.9 percent of the suburban population in Northeastern SMSA's over one million is black, while only 1.7 percent of the suburban population in SMSA's under one million is black. Black percentage representation increased far more rapidly between 1970 and 1977 in Northeastern SMSA's under one million than in those exceeding one million (Exhibit 5).

North Central: Between 1970 and 1977, this region's rate of black suburbanization slightly exceeded the nation's overall. In these years the black suburban population increased by 211,000, or 38.4 percent. As in the Northeast, this rate was higher in the suburbs of SMSA's having fewer than one million (56.1 percent) than in suburbs of SMSA's over one million (34.2 percent), though the difference between these two rates was not as great as in the Northeast (Exhibit 3).

In these years, net black migration has been irregular in both scale and mix. Between 1970 and 1975, there was a net black loss due to migration of 52,000 and in-migration was 74 percent of out-migration. During 1975-77, however, there occurred a net positive in-migration of 14,000, and in-migration amounted to 115 percent of those departing. This reversal is unexpected though small (Exhibit 4). In this region, blacks constitute just 8.7 percent of the total population (1977), but they amount to 34.8 percent of the population in the central cities of the larger SMSA's and 13.9 percent of

EXHIBIT 5

BLACKS AS PERCENT OF TOTAL POPULATION BY RESIDENCE AND REGION, 1977 AND 1970

(Percentages)

| | METROPOLITAN AREAS¹ OF | | | | | NONMETROPOLITAN AREAS | | |
| | 1,000,000 or more | | Less than 1,000,000 | | | | | |
	In Central Cities	Not in Central Cities	In Central Cities	Not in Central Cities	Total	In counties with a place of 25,000 or more	In counties without a place of 25,000 or more	Counties designated metropolitan since 1970²
NORTHEAST								
1977	25.5	4.9	9.9	1.7	1.5	2.6	0.4	4.6
1970	23.7	4.7	9.3	1.2	1.8	2.7	1.0	3.6
NORTH CENTRAL								
1977	34.8	4.2	13.9	2.0	1.9	5.3	1.1	5.5
1970	29.8	3.5	11.7	1.4	1.4	2.6	1.1	1.5
WEST								
1977	14.9	4.9	4.6	2.3	0.8	1.9	0.5	1.0
1970	12.4	3.5	4.4	1.7	1.1	1.4	1.0	1.7
SOUTH								
1977	39.9	10.8	24.6	11.2	19.1	18.6	19.3	12.7
1970	38.2	7.5	22.6	12.1	19.1	15.9	19.9	13.1

Notes: 1. For the 243 SMSA's (Standard Metropolitan Statistical Area) identified in the 1970 Census, according to 1970 boundaries.
2. These counties are also included in preceding three columns.

Source: U.S. Bureau of the Census, *Current Population Reports*, Series P-23, No. 75 "Social and Economic Characteristics of the Metropolitan and Nonmetropolitan Population: 1977 and 1970" (Washington, D.C.: U.S. Government Printing Office, 1978), Table 3.

the central city population in smaller SMSA's. Both figures exceed those of the Northeast and have risen more rapidly since 1970 (Exhibit 5).

This region is beset by many of the same urban problems as the Northeast. In recent years its smaller metropolitan areas have grown somewhat more rapidly than its larger ones, though in the aggregate its metropolitan areas have experienced substantial net-migration losses which have selectively altered both the supply of and the demand for suburban housing. The net impact of these regional trends has been a gradual increase in the proportion of the suburban population of the larger SMSA's which is black, from 3.5 percent in 1970 to 4.2 percent in 1977. Comparable black proportions in suburbs of SMSA's under one million total population were 1.4 in 1970 rising to 2.0 in 1977.

South: Here the number of suburban blacks increased by 279,000, or 61.2 percent during the period from 1970 to 1977. This was the highest rate for any of the major national regions, but it was applied to the smallest initial base of all regions in 1970. The South is in many respects unique, not only because of its role in black American history, but also due to the current, disproportionate size of its black population.

In 1977, 32 percent of the American population and 54 percent of the national black population lived in the South. And, as previously noted, a larger proportion of southern blacks (44.3 percent) resided in nonmetropolitan areas than did those in any other region in 1977. Likewise, the South was the only region in which fewer than half of all blacks (38.5 percent) resided in central cities in 1977. Ironically, however, southern blacks constitute larger fractions of total central city populations in both larger SMSA's (39.9 percent) and smaller SMSA's (24.6 percent) than in their equivalents in all other regions in 1977 (Exhibit 5).

While black suburbanizatiom proceeded more rapidly in the South than in all other regions during 1970-77, the fraction of all southern blacks residing in suburbs was smaller (17.2 percent) in 1977, than in all other regions except the North Central (15.2 percent). Most southern suburban blacks reside in SMSA's whose total population exceeds one million (613,000, 1977), while predictably fewer reside in the suburbs of SMSA's having fewer than one million total population (122,000, 1977). Both suburban categories experienced similar rates of black suburban increase during 1970-77 (Exhibit 3). It is also surprising that blacks constitute a larger fraction of the total suburban population in the South than in any other region. In 1977, 10.8 percent of all persons residing in the suburbs of SMSA's having total populations over one million were black. This is more than twice the rate for any other region. Similarly, 11.2 percent of the total population in 1977 of southern suburbs in SMSA's having fewer than one million was black. The West would be the next highest in this category, but it has just 2.3 percent (Exhibit 5).

Three factors bear the primary responsibility for these anomalous demographic conditions. First, the South has historically been "nonmetropolitan" in character. In 1977, the percent of all blacks residing outside metropolitan areas was almost the same as for the population at large. Second, blacks are over-represented in the South. Consequently it would be expected that they would have higher proportional representation in suburbs in the South than elsewhere. Third, since 1960, the South has increased in population by nearly one-fourth, a rate exceeded only in the West. During the 1960's, natural increase contributed over eight new persons for every one due to net in-migration. In the first half of the 1970's, natural increase and net migration contributed about equal numbers of new persons. From 1965 to 1970, there was a net out-migration of blacks from the South of 217,000; but from 1970 to 1977 there has been a net black gain through migration of 31,000 (Exhibit 4). Rising economic prosperity in the last decade has not only drawn many wealthier blacks to southern suburbs from other national regions, but it has also enabled large numbers of blacks to move to the suburbs from other places within the South.

West: The West, which in 1977, had 18.1 percent of the American population but just 8.8 percent of the nation's black population, has by far the largest absolute number of suburban blacks in all regions. In 1970, 1,681,000 blacks lived in the suburbs of the SMSA's of the West. This number increased by 34.4 percent through 1977. Though this rate was about the equivalent for the nation's blacks as a whole, the absolute increase was about the equal of that in all other regions combined.

The West is unique in several respects. There are not only fewer blacks in the West than in any other region, but they constitute only 5.6 percent (1977) of the total population in the region and are therefore proportionately less well represented here than in any other region. Unlike all other regions, the majority of the suburban blacks of the West reside in the suburbs of SMSA's having fewer than one million population.

In 1970, 66 percent of all suburban blacks of the region resided in this class of suburb. But since 1970, the black population of suburbs having in excess of one million people has grown extremely rapidly. From 1970 to 1977, the black population of the suburbs in these larger SMSA's grew by 83 percent, while the black population of the suburbs in the smaller SMSA's grew by just 9.6 percent (Exhibit 3). If current trends continue, the black population of the larger SMSA's very soon will exceed that in the suburbs of the smaller SMSA's.

The rapid growth of the black population in the suburbs of the larger SMSA's of the West is one measure of the particularly strong economies of these metropolitan areas. This in turn, has drawn to these suburbs many blacks from elsewhere within the region and from outside the region. Since 1965, the ratio of in- to out-migration of blacks has been much higher in the West than anywhere else. Between 1965 and 1977, the West experienced the net in-migration of 262,000 blacks. Not only was the figure far greater than for any other region, but the annual rate of net in-migration of blacks is rapidly accelerating (Exhibit 4). Since many of these will be prosperous, continued growth of the black suburban population seems assured. Considerably more growth in the region's black population would still have to occur before the proportion of the metropolitan population of the West which is black rivals the other regions'. In 1977, just 14.9 percent of the population of the central cities in the SMSA's of the West having in excess of one million inhabitants was black, and the proportion of the suburbs of the remaining, smaller SMSA's was still lower (4.6 percent) (Exhibit 5). Still, the proportion of the suburban population overall that is black is higher in the West than in any other region except the South. It is all the more noteworthy since the black population amounts to just under ten percent of the total population in the West, while it is about one-fourth of the total in the South.

Conclusions

There are very substantial differences among the major subnational regions regarding both the shape and pace of black suburbanization. These undoubtedly reflect differences in regional history which have generated divergent paths of urban spatial development. But within this broad-scale differentiation, there are still other pertinent differentials associated with the demographic, economic and attitudinal profiles of blacks and whites. History, pattern and profile combine to produce distinctive varieties of black suburbanization among the major regions of the nation. In the broadest sense, the rudiments of the process are everywhere the same, but differences in context, motivation and rationale require varied policy responses.

NOTES

1. The four major census regions are: *Northeast—Conneticut, Maine, Massachusetts, New Hampshire, New Jersey, New York, Pennsylvania, Rhode Island,* and *Vermont*; *North Central—Illinois, Indiana, Iowa, Kansas, Michigan, Minnesota, Missouri, Nebraska, North Dakota, Ohio, South Dakota,* and *Wisconsin*; *South—Alabama, Arkansas, Delaware, District of Columbia, Florida, Georgia, Kentucky, Louisiana, Maryland, Mississippi, North Carolina, Oklahoma, South Carolina, Tenssessee, Texas, Virginia,* and *West Virginia*; and *West—Alaska, Arizona, California, Colorado, Hawaii, Idaho, Montana, Nevada, New Mexico, Oregon, Utah, Washington,* and *Wyoming.*

2. About 5.6 million blacks live in the central cities of the SMSA's of the Northeast and North Central states having over one million total population. This amounts to 23.0 percent of the national black population in 1977.

3. All the data presented pertain to the 243 SMSA's identified and bounded in 1970. These are listed with their constituent counties in the 1970 Census of Population, Volume 1, U.S. Summary, Table 32. Note, however, that central city annexations since 1970 have shifted some suburban area and population to the central cities. While annexation has been extensive in some cities, the impact on regional totals regarding black suburbanization has been slight.

4. During the period from 1960 to 1970, the number of blacks in these same suburban areas increased from 2,675,000 to 3,433,000, or 28.3 percent. The average annual (compounded) rate of change has consequently been somewhat higher since 1970.

5

Black Suburbanization in Selected Metropolitan Areas

Black suburbanization in the nation's largest metropolitan centers tends to reflect the conditions of the major geographic regions in which these centers reside. To assess the dynamics of black suburbanization at this scale, twelve representative centers have been chosen for closer examination (Exhibit 6). Together, these twelve metropolitan areas account for over one-tenth of the national metropolitan population and about one in eight of all blacks residing in metropolitan areas. Rates of black suburbanization have been estimated for each center for the interval from 1970 to 1974 or 1975 or 1976, as indicated.

Metropolitan Overview

Boston, Philadelphia and New York: The Northeast. These three metropolitan centers of the Northeast experienced the lowest rates of black suburbanization of any of the twelve cases documented. By mid-decade, however, there were substantial differences among them regarding the rates of black homeownership in suburbs. Over half of Philadelphia's suburban black households owned their own homes while the level was far lower in Boston and New York. In all cases the fraction of all suburban households which were black was less than one in sixteen. Philadelphia is also distinctive in another respect. There, about one in three central city households is black, while the black proportion is far lower in Boston (16.8 percent) and New York (8.9 percent).

Detroit, Chicago and St. Louis: The North Central Region. In these three centers of the North Central region, considerably higher rates of black suburbanization are found than in the three centers of the Northeast examined earlier. St. Louis experienced an increase in black suburban households of nearly 60 percent, while Chicago was second at 46 percent and Detroit was third at 32 percent. St. Louis's high suburbanization rate is undoubtedly partly due to central city decline, documented in a 6.4 percent loss in black central city households from 1970 to 1976. There were proportionately fewer black households in the central city of St. Louis (just 14.5 percent) than in either Chicago (33.0 percent) or Detroit (47.4 percent). Overall, the rate of black homeownership in suburbs was comparably high in all SMSA's except those of the eastern seaboard (Boston, New York and Washington, D.C.) (Exhibit 6).

Washington, D.C., Atlanta and Houston: The South. The centers of South examined are a diverse lot. Two of the three realized extremely high rates of black suburbanization: Atlanta (132 percent) and Washington, D.C. (89 percent). Houston, however, lagged behind despite its recent prosperity. This city also was distinctive in having proportionately very few black central city households (just 7 percent of all central city households) (Exhibit 6).[1]

Los Angeles-Long Beach, San Francisco-Oakland and Seattle-Everett: The West. Of these three western centers, Seattle-Everett is unique in having extremely few numbers of black households in both its central cities and in its suburbs. Seattle-Everett's 144 percent increase in the number of suburban black households between 1970 and 1976 is therefore numerically insignificant. Los Angeles-Long Beach is a more important case. There, the number of black households is far larger, though just 15 percent of all households in its central cities, and 7 percent in it suburbs, were black. Overall, the number of suburban black households in Los Angeles-Long Beach increased by almost 50 percent from 1970 to 1974, while the comparable figure for San Francisco-Oakland was 25 percent during 1970-75 (Exhibit 6).

EXHIBIT 6

BLACK SUBURBANIZATION IN SELECTED MAJOR METROPOLITAN AREAS BY RESIDENCE, 1970 TO 1974, 5 OR 6[1]

(Numbers are rounded to nearest thousand, except percentages)

	CENTRAL CITY BLACK HOUSEHOLDS[3]				SUBURBS[4] BLACK HOUSEHOLDS[3]				
SMSA AND REGION[2]	1970	1974,5,6	Percent change 1970-1974,5,6	Percent of all households black in 1974,5,6	1970	1974,5,6	Percent change 1970-1974,5,6	Percent of all households black in 1974,5,6	Percent of black units owner-occupied in 1974,5,6
A. 1970-1974									
(NE) Boston	32	34	6.3	16.8	6	8	25.4	1.2	29.1
(NC) Detroit	193	220	14.2	47.4	25	32	31.8	3.7	59.8
(W) Los Angeles-Long Beach	177	181	2.6	15.2	64	95	48.4	7.1	56.2
(S) Washington, D.C.	164	169	3.3	65.7	41	78	89.0	10.7	38.3
B. 1970-1975									
(S) Atlanta	71	82	14.8	55.0	13	31	131.6	8.6	52.6
(NC) Chicago	313	353	12.6	33.0	31	45	45.9	3.7	53.2
(NE) Philadelphia	195	204	4.3	31.2	49	62	26.2	6.4	50.4
(W) San Francisco-Oakland	72	88	21.5	18.9	32	40	25.3	5.0	45.0
C. 1970-1976									
(S) Houston	90	112	24.2	7.1	17	23	35.3	2.3	68.1
(NE) New York	523	611	17.0	8.9	56	71	27.7	1.9	18.3
(NC) St. Louis	73	68	-6.4	14.5	33	53	59.3	3.0	58.8
(W) Seattle-Everett	13	16	28.6	3.2	1	2	144.4	0.2	51.3

Notes: 1. Based on samples of 15,000 housing units in each SMSA, divided equally between central city and non-central city portions of SMSA's.
2. SMSA's are defined according to constant boundaries as of 1971. Regional designations = Northeast (NE), North Central (NC), South (S), and West (W).
3. Each occupied housing unit is assumed to be occupied by one household having a black household head.
4. Suburbs are the portion of SMSA's outside central cities.

Source: U.S. Department of Commerce, Bureau of the Census, *Current Housing Reports*, Series H-170-74 (Numbers 3, 5, 7, 18), H-170-75 (Numbers 21, 22, 33, 39), H-170-76 (Numbers 49, 53, 59, 60), Housing Characteristics for Selected Metropolitan Areas (Washington, D.C.: U.S. Government Printing Office, 1976, 1977 and 1978).

The Correlates of Black Suburbanization

In an effort to assess the similarities and differences among the twelve metropolitan centers for which detailed information is available and to determine whether distinct regional types of black suburbanization exist, a number of correlates of suburbanization have been examined graphically (Exhibit 7). Expectations (hypotheses) regarding each of these correlates as well as discussion of the empirical evidence in each instance are presented below:

The "Push" Factor: Black Population in the Central City (Exhibit 7-A).

Expectations: The rate of black suburbanization since 1970 would be expected to be higher, the greater the absolute number of black households residing in the central city (or cities) of the metropolitan area. This is because the initial 1970 base year black suburban population would be expected to be more or less proportionate to the black population in the central city in that same year, and because the larger the number of black central city residents, the greater would be the pace at which the move to the suburbs would accelerate. The greater the number of suburban black newcomers, the easier it may be for others to follow. The process is circular, cumulative and prone to accelerate.[2]

Evidence: These expectations are confirmed only partially by the evidence (See Exhibit 7-A). Among the twelve areas examined no strong, positive relationship emerges. The metropolitan areas having smaller central city black populations, excepting Seattle-Everett, Atlanta, and Washington, D.C. (circled in 7-A) are irregularly scattered. Chicago and New York, furthermore, seem to have had slower rates of black suburbanization than they might have been expected to have.[3]

Spillover: The Proportion of the Central City Population Which Is Black (Exhibit 7-B).

Expectation: The higher the proportion of the central city population that is black, the higher the expected rate of black suburbanization. This is because the greater the proportion of the central city population that is black, the greater the propensity to "spillover" into the suburbs, and generally, all other things equal, we would expect that "spillover" into contiguous areas would occur more rapidly than "leap-frogging" into non-adjacent areas.[4]

Evidence: Here the empirical evidence gives moderate support (See Exhibit 7-B). Atlanta and Washington, D.C. seem supportive

EXHIBIT 7

Selected Correlates of Black Suburbanization in Twelve Major
Metropolitan Centers[1], 1970 To Mid-Decade

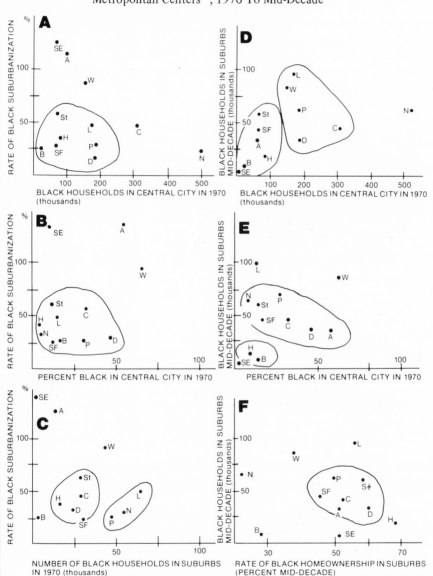

Notes: 1. These twelve centers are: Atlanta (A), Boston (B), Chicago (C), Detroit (D), Houston (H), Los Angeles-Long Beach (L), New York (N), Philadelphia (P), St. Louis (St.), San Francisco-Oakland (SF), Seattle-Everett (SE), and Washington, D.C. (W).

       2. The encircled point clusters are visual judgements intended to assist in the interpretation of each scattergram.

Source: See Exhibit 6.

of this hypothesis, but Philadelphia and Detroit do not. Seattle-Everett is really a distinct class because of the small number of blacks residing there.

The "Pull" Factor: Black Suburban Path-breakers (Exhibit 7-C)

Expectations: The rate of black suburbanization since 1970 would be expected to be directly related to the absolute number of black households residing in suburbs in 1970, in general.

Evidence: The reality is that, excepting Atlanta and Seattle-Everett, there is some indication of a weak, positive relationship between the magnitude of the suburban black population at the beginning of the decade, and the rate of increase since that time. The responsiveness of the suburbanization rate to the initial black suburban population in 1970, varied widely among metro-politan areas. Washington, D.C., St. Louis, Chicago, Houston and Boston would appear to have had rates of increase which were somewhat above the level which might have been expected, whereas Detroit, San Francisco, Philadelphia, New York and Los Angeles-Long Beach had rates which were perhaps somewhat less than would have been expected. Of course, this is a small sample on which to base these observations.

A number of ancillary factors surely complicate the relation-ship between these two variables. These include the nature and residential condition of the black households who initially resided within the suburban ring, the proportionate representation of the initial black suburban population within the suburban ring as a whole and within the particular suburban municipalities in which they were most prevalent, and other factors associated with the social and economic characteristics of the pool of potential black migrants destined for suburban localities.

A "Push" Factor Variant (Exhibit 7-D)

Expectations: A direct, positive relationship would be expected between the number of black households residing in central cities in 1970, and the number of black households residing in the suburban ring by mid-decade.

Evidence: These expectations are at least partially confirmed by the evidence. New York, Chicago, Detroit and Houston appear to have somewhat smaller black suburban populations by mid-decade than their black central city populations in 1970 might have indicated. In general, however, a positive association between these two variables does seem to exist. This would suggest perhaps, that a major controlling factor is the magnitude of the black

Final Observations

This Chapter has examined the conditions of black suburbanization in selected metropolitan centers across the nation. Initially, to examine the proposition that there exist observable differences in the pace and character of black suburbanization among the major subnational regions, we grouped these large metropolitan centers by region. While there do appear to be some differences among regions largely due to the absolute scale of the black population and the conditions of "sending" areas (central cities) and "receiving areas" (the suburban realm), there also appear to be equally significant differences among metropolitan centers within regions. That is, the "within" variation seemed to be as great as the "between" variation. This finding of course, pertains only to these larger metropolitan areas. And many important regional distinctions reflect system behavior over a more extensive range of center sizes. This is particularly true of the South and West, regions that have highly distinctive racial histories and patterns, as demonstrated in the previous chapter.

Seeking to isolate more precisely the common dimensions of the suburbanization process among these selected metropolitan centers, the Chapter subsequently examined several distinct hypotheses regarding the determining correlates of black suburbanization. For each, a scattergram was presented showing the position of each center in relation to all others. And each was examined to discern the existence of a patterned relationship between the chosen measure of black suburbanization and the hypothesized correlate. While certain of the hypothesized relationships derived some measure of support from these data, many others did not. In fact there tended to emerge distinct center clusters relative to each relationship, but the identity of the centers in these clusters was different among scattergrams. This suggests that black suburbanization is a highly complex process indeed, and that much of the residual variation in this sample of major centers can be explained only by incorporating additional variables into the analysis. Among these would be measures of metropolitan shape, pattern and scale, propulsive and exclusionary forces at work within the area, and social and economic dimensions of the demographic profiles of blacks and whites.

NOTES

1. The Washington, D.C. area is also examined in Eunice Grier and George Grier, "Black Suburbanization at the Mid-1970's" (Washington, D.C.:

Washington Center for Metropolitan Studies, April 1978).

2. For an examination of this process see L.K. Norwood and E.A.T. Barth, "Urban Desegregation: Negro Pioneers and Their White Neighbors," in *End of Innocence: A Suburban Reader,* edited by C.M.Haar (Glenview, Illinois: Scott, Foresman, 1972), 118-123; W.A.V. Clark, "Patterns of Black Intraurban Mobility and Restricted Relocation Opportunities," in *Perspectives in Geography 2: Geography of the Ghetto,* edited by Harold M. Rose (DeKalb: Northern Illinois University Press, 1972).

3. It might be argued that only those SMSA's whose end year (1974, 5 or 6) is the same should be compared. In fact, the picture is hardly more clear when this is done.

4. See Richard Morrill, "The Negro Ghetto: Problems and Alternatives," *Geographic Review,* Vol. 55 (1965), 339-61; Richard L. Morrill, "A Geographic Perspective of the Black Ghetto," in *Perspectives in Geography 2: Geography of the Ghetto,* edited by Harold M. Rose (DeKalb: Northern Illinois University Press, 1972); and Harold Rose, "Development of an Urban Sub-system: the Case of the American Ghetto," *Annals of the Association of American Geographers,* Vol. 60 (1970), 1-17.

6

The Impact of Migration on the Development of the Black Population in Suburbs

$\mathbf{M}$igration has been the primary determinant of demographic change within the black population residing in suburbs in recent years.[1] Over ninety percent of the increase in the national black suburban population between 1970 and 1978 (1,179,000 persons) was due to the net effect of migration to and from suburbs. Just 82,000 of this total increase was due to net natural increase. Most suburban blacks, therefore, are relative newcomers.

The Components of Black Migration: Interregional Differentials

Black suburbanization is not however, a simple function of the intra-metropolitan movement of blacks from central cities to suburbs, as it has been characterized so often. Rather, the migration component of black suburban change is quite complex, interweaving two-way flows within a national matrix of origins and destinations. The evidence of black migration to, from and within suburbs from 1970 to 1975 and from 1975 to 1978, is assembled in Exhibit 8.[2]

EXHIBIT 8
BLACK MIGRATION TO, FROM AND WITHIN SUBURBS,
BY REGION, 1970 TO 1978

(Numbers in thousands, except percent of total black population
in suburbs in parentheses)

1970 To 1975[1]

Population at end of period	United States	Northeast	North Central	South	West
Black population in suburbs	3,648	849	677	1,608	514
Nonmovers in suburbs	1,686	404	346	784	152
Movers residing in suburbs	1,962	445	331	824	362
Total moving within suburbs	794	254	144	218	178
	(22%)	(30%)	(21%)	(14%)	(35%)
Same SMSA	705	215	126	202	162
Different SMSA	89	39	18	16	16
Total moving to suburbs	1,168	190	184	611	183
	(32%)	(22%)	(27%)	(38%)	(36%)
From central city:					
Same SMSA	524	81	29	281	133
Different SMSA	194	61	49	70	14
From non-metro areas	109	14	29	57	9
From abroad[3]	341	34	77	203	27
Total moving from suburbs[4]	446	106	72	179	89
	(12%)	(12%)	(11%)	(11%)	(17%)
To central city:					
Same SMSA	234	49	30	102	53
Different SMSA	148	45	32	41	30
To non-metro areas	64	12	10	36	6
Net migration to suburbs	525	84	112	432	94
	(15%)	(10%)	(17%)	(27%)	(18%)

Notes: 1. Persons five years of age and over in 1975. The interval begins and ends in March.

2. Persons five years of age and over in 1978. The interval begins and ends in March.

3. The total number from abroad in suburbs by 1975 is given in *Current Population Report*, Series P-20, No. 285, Table 28.

4. Migration from suburbs to areas abroad is not available, and therefore excluded.

(continued on next page)

EXHIBIT 8 (cont'd)

1975 TO 1978[2]

Population at end of period	United States	Northeast	North Central	South	West
Black population in suburbs	4,612	827	806	2,314	665
Nonmovers in suburbs	2,667	517	445	1,386	319
Movers residing in suburbs	1,945	310	361	928	346
Total moving within suburbs	897	210	147	400	140
	(19%)	(25%)	(18%)	(17%)	(21%)
Same SMSA	801	159	140	376	126
Different SMSA	96	51	7	24	14
Total moving to suburbs	1,050	100	215	528	207
	(23%)	(12%)	(27%)	(23%)	(31%)
From central city:					
Same SMSA	546	30	141	274	101
Different SMSA	234	57	21	72	84
From non-metro areas	159	6	46	93	14
From abroad[3]	111	7	7	89	8
Total moving from suburbs[4]	478	113	77	193	95
	(10%)	(14%)	(10%)	(8%)	(14%)
To central city:					
Same SMSA	261	55	34	113	59
Different SMSA	148	45	32	41	30
To non-metro areas	69	13	11	39	6
Net migration to suburbs	572	−13	138	335	112
	(12%)	(−2%)	(17%)	(14%)	(17%)

Source: U.S. Bureau of the Census, *Current Population Reports*, Series P-20, No. 285, "Mobility of the Population of the United States, March 1970 to March 1975," (Washington, D.C.: U.S. Government Printing Office, 1975), Table 1, 28; and Series P-20, No. 331, "Geographical Mobility: March 1975 to March 1978," (Washington, D.C.: U.S. Government Printing Office, November, 1978), Table 39. Persons moving to, from and within suburbs by region for 1970-75 are estimated by the author based on *Annual Housing Survey* migration data for 1975, plus *Current Population Reports* estimates for all national categories and regional totals for 1970-75.

A "migrant" is one whose address changed between the start and end of the given time interval. Since intermediate moves are ignored, it is not appropriate to add together migrations in the two time intervals. During 1970 to 1975, there was a net migration of over one-half million blacks to suburbs. This was the equivalent of 15 percent of the national black suburban population in 1975 which was 3,648,000. By 1978, 4,612,000 blacks lived in suburbs, and from 1975 to 1978, net migration contributed again over one-half million black persons to suburbs. The absolute and percentage contribution of net migration has varied significantly among regions.

During 1970-75, the greatest net migration gain was the South's, amounting to 432,000 persons, or 27 percent of the total black suburban population in the South at the end of this first interval. In contrast, the Northeast experienced the lowest absolute (84,000) and relative (10 percent) gain of all regions during the interval. From 1975 to 1978, the picture had changed dramatically. The rank order of absolute regional net migration gains remained the same, but the overall national rate of annual net migration increase was appreciably higher. But while the annual rate of increase due to net migration increased from 1970-75 to 1975-78 in the North Central and West regions, it fell slightly in the South and more so in the Northeast. In the Northeast there was in fact an absolute population loss due to net migration during 1975-78 (Exhibit 8).

Temporal Variation in the Composition of Migration Flows

Not only have the rates of net migration varied over time and among regions, but so has the composition of migration flows producing these net effects (Exhibit 8).[3]

Moves to Suburbs

About one-half of all moves by blacks to suburbs (52 percent, 1975-78) originate in the central city of the same SMSA, while one-fifth (22 percent, 1975-78) originate in the central cities of other SMSA's, and an additional 15 percent originate in nonmetropolitan areas. Surprisingly, 11 percent of all such moves originated abroad, and during 1970-75, this category constituted 29 percent of the total moving to suburbs. There is considerable shifting within and among suburban areas, as well, and this is apparently increasing. Among regions the relative contribution of these migrant sources varied widely (Exhibit 8).

Moves from Suburbs

Surprisingly, for every 2.2 black persons moving to suburbs from non-suburban areas, one will move out. During 1975-78, this amounted to an out-flow of 478,000 persons, 55 percent of whom went to the central city of the same SMSA, and 31 percent went to the central cities of other SMSA's, while the remainder (14 percent) went to nonmetropolitan areas. Regarding the migration exchange between central cities and suburbs, during 1975-78, 780,000 black persons moved from central cities to suburbs, while 409,000 followed a reverse path. So despite this large number of moves between central cities and suburbs, the net suburban gain was just 371,000.

Migration between suburbs and nonmetropolitan areas, in contrast , is in approximate balance. During 1975-78, the net suburban gain in this exchange of migrants was just 11,000. There is evidence that this balance is gradually shifting in favor of nonmetropolitan areas, possibly due to the movement of blacks to areas just beyond the metropolitan perimeter to secure less expensive accommodations, or to take advantage of the new employment opportunities that have arisen in recent years not only in the suburbs but in nonmetropolitan areas as well. There is substantial variation in the proportional distribution of the destinations of out-migrants from suburbs among regions (Exhibit 8).[4]

Race, Migration and Welfare

It is popularly asserted that black suburbanization is indicative of improving conditions for black Americans. Certainly for many the move to the suburbs reflects growing prosperity, and for some the move to new low-rent suburban housing will lead to improved residential conditions and employment opportunities. For still others, however, the suburban reality does not equal the idealized perception. These are people residing in the older, inner-ring suburbs whose conditions may differ little from those in central cities. These, as well, are black people living in poverty pockets of more prosperous suburbs and in the older outer suburbs which were once functionally remote from the central cities but which today may be incorporated within SMSA's. They are "suburban" by statistical quirk, though as these outlying communities are enveloped by the metropolitan region some undoubtedly do become more suburban in character.

In recent years the gap between black and white incomes has begun to close though the rate of convergence differs substantially among

EXHIBIT 9
MEDIAN INCOME, PERSONS 14 YEARS OLD AND OVER BY RACE, SEX, AND METROPOLITAN SIZE AND STATUS, 1975
(Dollars)[1]

| | IN METROPOLITAN AREAS OF | | | | OUTSIDE METROPOLITAN AREAS | |
| | 1,000,000 or more | | Under 100,000 | | | |
MEDIAN INCOME	In Central Cities	Outside Central Cities	In Central Cities	Outside Central Cities	Nonfarm	Farm
	(black/white income ratios given as decimal fractions)					
Males:						
All Workers						
Black	.71	.69	.64	.63		
	6,728	7,987	5,756	6,328	4,001	2,597
White	9,410	11,519	9,044	10,042	8,043	6,057
Year-Round, Full-Time Workers						
Black	.81	.70	.78	.69		
	11,159	10,998	10,133	9,412	6,781	B
Percent of all	45	51	43	49	37	36
White	13,800	15,736	13,041	13,738	11,820	8,601
Percent of all	52	57	53	57	50	62

Notes: B = Base less than 75,000.
1. Persons fourteen years old and over as of March 1976, excluding civilian institutional population and armed forces personnel living without families on post.

EXHIBIT 9 (con't)

MEDIAN INCOME, PERSONS 14 YEARS OLD AND OVER BY RACE, SEX, AND METROPOLITAN SIZE AND STATUS, 1975

(Dollars)[1]

| | *IN METROPOLITAN AREAS OF* | | | | *OUTSIDE METROPOLITAN AREAS* | |
| | *1,000,000 or more* | | *Under 100,000* | | | |
	In Central Cities	*Outside Central Cities*	*In Central Cities*	*Outside Central Cities*	*Nonfarm*	*Farm*
	(black/white income ratios given as decimal fractions)					
MEDIAN INCOME						
Females:						
All Workers	.95	1.21	.74	.75		
Black	3,842	4,622	2,814	2,553	2,219	1,367
White	4,042	3,816	3,789	3,409	2,950	2,229
Year-Round, Full-Time Workers	.94	1.04	.88	.82		
Black	8,146	9,039	6,820	6,250	5,176	B
Percent of all	32	40	28	34		
White	8,641	8,691	7,755	7,628	6,606	5,804
Percent of all	31	30	30	30	25	25

Source: U.S. Bureau of the Census, *Current Population Reports,* Series P-60, No. 105, "Money Income in 1975 of Families and Persons in the United States," (Washington, D.C.: U.S. Government Printing Office, 1977), Table 41.

various categories of wage earners. The rate has tended to converge at a faster pace when wage differentials in comparable jobs in the same industry are examined. But the gap has closed more slowly, if at all, with respect to more diverse segments of the black and white populations.[5] In 1975, the median income of black men and women residing in central cities and in suburbs was less than that of their white counterparts, regardless of the size of the metropolitan area, with one exception. Black women residing in suburbs within metropolitan areas of over one million persons had a higher median income than comparable whites in this year (Exhibit 9). The crucial issue is not now "comparable pay for comparable work", but equal access to preferred employment opportunities.

Regardless of place of residence (central city or suburbs) or size of metropolitan area, the black-to-white ratio of median incomes was lower in 1975 for black men than women, but the differential was greater in suburbs than in central cities (Exhibit 9). Surprisingly, the black-to-white ratio of median incomes was actually lower in suburbs than central cities, regardless of the size of the metropolitan area in this year.[6] The reverse held true for women in larger metropolitan areas (exceeding one million population). There suburban black women earned more than comparable whites, but in central cities black women earned just slightly less than whites. In smaller metropolitan areas, however, not only did black women earn less than their white counterparts, regardless of place of residence, but those working full-time year-round had incomes which were a higher fraction of those of white women in central cities than in suburbs.

Overall, among year-round, full-time workers, whites earned higher median incomes in suburbs than in central cities, regardless of sex, except in the case of women in metropolitan areas of under one million persons. In the same year, blacks regardless of sex earned higher median incomes in central cities than in suburbs, except in the case of women residing in the larger metropolitan areas (Exhibit 8). Of course, these figures measure income by place of residence not work, and there is a significant flow of commuters both ways between central cities and suburbs.

Comparison of Family versus Individual Incomes of Suburban Blacks

A significantly different picture emerges when family rather than individual income trends in suburbs are examined. Between 1970 and 1976, the median income of black suburban families in constant 1976 dollars rose by 12 percent to $12,037 as the number of these families increased by 54 percent (Exhibit 10). In these same years the

EXHIBIT 10

BLACK FAMILY INCOME DISTRIBUTION IN CENTRAL CITIES AND SUBURBS, 1976 AND 1970

(In constant 1976 dollars. Families as of March 1977 and April 1970 in thousands)

TOTAL MONEY INCOME	SUBURBS				CENTRAL CITIES			
	1976		*1970*		*1976*		*1970*	
	Number	Percent	Number	Percent	Number	Percent	Number	Percent
$0 to 2,999	81	7.1	95	12.7	307	9.5	375	12.8
3,000 to 5,999	176	15.3	107	14.3	742	22.9	464	15.9
6,000 to 9,999	225	19.6	144	19.3	666	20.5	594	20.3
10,000 to 14,999	176	15.3	161	21.7	479	14.8	645	22.1
15,000 to 24,999	348	30.3	182	24.4	828	25.5	644	22.1
25,000 and over	141	12.4	57	7.6	220	6.8	197	6.7
TOTAL FAMILIES	1,147	100.0	746	100.0	3,242	100.0	2,919	100.0
MEDIAN INCOME (DOLLARS)	12,037		10,745		9,361		10,188	
MEAN INCOME (DOLLARS)	13,727		12,245		11,398		11,712	

Source: U.S. Bureau of the Census, *Current Population Reports*, Series P-23, No. 75, "Social and Economic Characteristics of the Metropolitan and Nonmetropolitan Population: 1977 and 1970" (Washington, D.C.: U.S. Government Printing Office, 1978), Table 20.

median income of black central city families was actually falling by 8 percent to $9,361. At the same time, the number of black suburban families earning $15,000 or more increased by 105 percent to 489,000, while those earning less than this amount increased by just 30 percent to 658,000 families. Both the absolute and percentage increases in the first category exceeded those of the second. Despite the rapid increase in the number of wealthier black families in suburbs, there remained a large difference between the median incomes of black and white suburban families. In 1976, the median income of white suburban families was $17,371, exceeding the black counterpart by 44 percent. In that year 62 percent of all white suburban families had incomes of $15,000 or more, in contrast to 43 percent for black families (Exhibit 10).

Family income, of course, is the sum of the incomes of all individual family members. Since there are important differences in family composition between black and white families, even in suburbs, direct comparisons based on family income may be somewhat misleading. Consequently, with respect to the incentive to move from central city to suburb, it may be more significant that black males working full-time, year-round earn lower median incomes in suburbs than central cities at least in the smaller metropolitan areas, than that black families have higher median incomes in suburbs than in central cities.

Median income, in any case, is a gross statistic incapable of contributing much insight into the motivations and experiences of the black suburban population. This is because the black suburban population is composed of many diverse elements to which the overall median relates. There are several major reasons, in fact, why median individual income might be higher in central cities than in suburbs. Undoubtedly, in central cities there are sizable numbers of moderate and even upper income black households whose presence elevates the median. And in some suburban areas there are significant poverty pockets almost indistinguishable from central city ghettos regarding the status quo of their population, if not their physical appearance.

Whatever the interpretation, however, it is clear that the central city-suburban income differential is in itself inadequate for evaluating the significance of black suburbanization. Movment of wealthier black households to suburbs reflects growing white suburban receptiveness whether or not newly arriving black households are dispersed or concentrated in particular areas or neighborhoods. For them, suburban residence will tend to mean better housing, neighborhoods and services than they might have been able to secure outside suburbs. The presence of poorer black households in suburbs is in part the historical status quo. Undoubtedly, a significant fraction of the newly arriving, poorer black households are drawn to the more impoverished suburban localities in both the inner-ring suburbs and in some outlying poverty pockets. Others, however, have been able to secure suburban dwellings as a more or less direct result of growing white receptiveness in more prosperous localities and neighborhoods where older housing has filtered down to within their financial reach and newer, lower-rent dwellings have been constructed. In general, it is consequently desirable to distinguish between less prosperous black households migrating to suburbs "unassisted" and those who move to suburbs from non-suburban areas as a more direct result of growing white receptiveness and the presence of quality dwellings which they can afford to rent. In a special sense these latter households are "assisted" and will probably tend to realize a greater gain in suburbanization than those unassisted. Of course, certain suburban areas which have been home for the unassisted migrants probably serve as staging areas from which black households will move as new opportunities arise and word of mouth convinces them that they would not encounter at least overt discrimination if they were to move to these more favored residences.

The Incomes of Movers and Nonmovers

Since 1970, net migration to suburbs probably has tended to increase the mean income of black suburban families of two or more persons. From 1970 to 1974, the mean income of black families moving to suburbs from central cities in the same metropolitan area was $10,567, while those moving from suburbs to central cities in the same metropolitan area had a mean income of $9,165 (Exhibit 11). Since the net gain due to moves between central cities and adjacent suburbs amounted to 55 percent of the total net migration gain in suburbs during 1970-75 (Exhibit 8), it is likely that the net migration of families during 1970-74 to suburbs from adjacent central cities was a primary determinant of change in mean suburban income. In fact, since the ratio of in- to out-migrating families was 1.67 during 1970-74, and the mean income of black suburban families which did not move during the period was $10,720, the impact of net migration was probably to increase the overall mean income of suburban black families.

During 1975-77, however, the situation had changed. In this second period the mean income of black families who resided in suburbs but did not move rose to $14,755. In these same years, the

EXHIBIT 11
MOBILITY STATUS OF THE BLACK POPULATION,
BY FAMILY STATUS AND INCOME, 1970-75 and 1975-77[1]

| | Total Persons[3] | | Families of Two or More | | | | Unrelated Individuals | | | |
| | 1970-75 | 1975-77 | 1970-74 | | 1975-77 | | 1970-74 | | 1975-77 | |
			Persons	Mean Family Income	Persons	Mean Family Income	Persons	Mean Income	Persons	Mean Income
Total Population (thousands)	21,377	23,559	19,354	$8,807	20,938	$11,276	2,183	$4,579	2,559	$5,475
Nonmovers (thousands)	10,217	17,100	11,331		15,502	11,812	1,085		1,598	5,485
Central Cities			NA	10,096	NA	12,175		4,378		5,796
Suburbs			NA	10,720	NA	14,755		3,860		6,743
Nonmetro. Areas			NA	6,752	NA	9,184		2,448		3,873

NA   Not available
(B)   Base less than 75,000

Notes: 1. Income data are for the period 1970-74, not 1970-75.
2. For example, during 1970-75, 9,778,000 blacks moved in all. This was 45.7 percent of 21,377,000 total blacks. Therefore, (45.7/5 years) = 9.1 percent of the total black population moved during *each* year of the period. This is the first percent given in column 1.
3. Total persons five years old or older for 1970-75, and persons two years old or older for 1975-7.

(continued on next page)

EXHIBIT 11 (con't)
MOBILITY STATUS OF THE BLACK POPULATION,
BY FAMILY STATUS AND INCOME, 1970-75 and 1975-77[1]

(Percent of Total in Column Head Moving Each Year)[2]

| | Total Persons[3] | | Families of Two or More | | | | Unrelated Individuals | | | |
| | | | 1970-74 | | 1975-77 | | 1970-74 | | 1975-77 | |
	1970-75	1975-77	Persons	Mean Family Income	Persons	Mean Family Income	Persons	Mean Income	Persons	Mean Income
Movers										
Within Same SMSA	9.1	13.5	9.5	$8,092	11.5	$9,883	10.8	$5,170	18.5	$5,455
In Central City	4.4	6.0	4.5	7,940	5.5	9,392	5.8	5,137	9.5	5,589
In Suburbs	.7	1.5	.8	9,468	1.5	11,769	.8	(B)	2.0	6,327
Central City to Suburbs	.5	1.0	.5	10,567	1.0	12,966	.8	(B)	1.0	(B)
Suburbs to Central City	.2	.5	.3	9,165	.5	(B)	.5	(B)	1.0	(B)
Between SMSA's	.8	1.5	.8	9,171	1.5	9,638	1.3	5,545	2.0	4,733
Nonmetro. to Metro.	.4	.5	.5	6,179	.5	(B)	.4	(B)	.5	(B)
Metro. to Nonmetro.	.3	.5	.3	(B)	.5	(B)	.3	(B)	.5	(B)
Nonmetro. to Nonmetro.	1.9	2.0	1.8	6,991	2.0	7,918	1.0	2,301	2.0	4,190

Source: U.S. Bureau of the Census, *Current Population Reports*, Series P-23, Nos. 55 and 75, "Social and Economic Characteristics of the Metropolitan and Nonmetropolitan Population," (Washington, D.C.: U.S. Government Printing Office, 1975 and 1978), Table 8; and series P-20, No. 285, "Mobility of the Population of the United States March 1970 to March 1975" (Washington, D.C.: U.S. Government Printing Office, 1975), Table 1.

mean income of black families moving from central cities to suburbs of the same metropolitan area also rose, but only to $12,966. Since in this period two migrants moved *to* the suburbs for every one who moved *from* the suburbs to the adjacent central city, it can be tentatively concluded that the effect of net migration to suburbs during 1975-77 was to diminish the overall mean income of black families. This cannot be absolutely confirmed however, because the mean income of black families moving from suburbs to adjacent central cities is not available and, in any case, comparable income data for all other migrant flows to and from suburbs is not available (Exhibit 11). Comparable income figures for unrelated individuals moving between central cities and adjacent suburbs are also not available, though related information is presented in Exhibit 11.

Final Observations

Black suburbanization is a spatial process in two dimensions. The first is the dynamic of black entry into the suburban realm. This dynamic is a highly complex interweaving of two-way migration flows within a national matrix of origins and destinations. The second is the dimension of movement within the suburban realm as the black household seeks to position itself within the interacting *opportunity structures* of work and residence. These two dimensions are interdependent.

The process of suburban entry may take any of several sequential forms. Residential entry may be preceded by the incorporation of certain suburban "nodes" within the household's daily "activity system". These nodes may be places of work, shopping or socializing. The most important, of course, is the workplace. For some, the acquisition of a job in the suburbs may be the first step in a sequence of displacements leading eventually to the household's securing a suburban residence. For others, a home in the suburbs may precede the displacement from central city to suburbs of the major non-residential place nodes within the household's activity system. This matter is further explored in later Chapters.

In the pre-suburban era of black metropolitan residence, the development of black residential sub-systems proceeded incrementally as blacks gradually enlarged their life-space by expanding the ghetto into contiguous areas within the central city. Most intra-migrations were of shorter distances, and penetration of white neighborhoods occurred selectively and with the gravitational inevitability of a ponderous glacier, or so it seemed to many. Occasionally, new ghetto nodes were "seeded" into urban space and the expansionary process would be initiated again. Overall, additional numbers of blacks were incorporated into the fabric of the central city by three distinct processes. These were ghetto expansion into contiguous areas, "seeding" of new black enclaves within the central city and "packing" at greater densities in existing enclaves. And "packing" was often the only option when the surrounding areas proved resistent to seeding or expansion.

Today, the incorporation of additional black population within the metropolitan region includes suburban residential opportunites. In some metropolitan areas the suburbanization of black residential opportunities will or has occurred through processes of residential expansion which are no different from those which once predominated only in central cities. Spillover into the inner suburbs of adjacent central city ghettos is, in fact, one pervasive dynamic of black suburbanization. With rising black incomes, the opening up of once all-white neighborhoods and workplaces and the gradual decline of overtly racial exclusionary practices, it now seems likely that a new and different process of residential patterning has begun to occur, not only in suburbs, but also in central cities. The fundamental fact remains, however, that the less prosperous black household remains far more constrained than its middle class counterpart.

NOTES

1. For an empirical overview of black-white mobility comparisons see Ronald J. McAllister, Edward J. Kaiser and Edgar W. Butler, "Residential Mobility of Blacks and Whites: A National Longitudinal Survey," *American Journal of Sociology* Vol. 77 (1972), 445-455. See also, William H. Frey, "Black Movement to the Suburbs: Potentials and Prospects for Metropolitan-wide Integration," Discussion Papers, No. 452-77 (Madison, Wisconsin: University of Wisconsin, Institute for Research on Poverty, December 1977); Harold X.Connally, "Black Movement to the Suburbs: Suburbs Doubling Their Black Populations During the 1960's,"*Urban Affairs Quarterly*, Vol. 9 (1973), 91-111; and Curtis C. Roseman and Prentice L. Knight III, "Residential Environment and Migration Behavior of Urban Blacks," *The Professional Geographer*, Vol. XXVII, No. 2 (May 1975), 160-65.

2. All the data in this Exhibit have been drawn from the *Current Population Reports* except for the *regional* migration tabulations for the interval 1970-75. For this period, all figures regarding migration *to* and *within* suburbs have been imputed from the national and regional (top three rows) estimates of these *Reports* plus information regarding the composition of regional flows for 1975, appearing in the publication *Annual Housing Survey: 1975—United States and Regions, Part D*, Series H-150-75D. The procedure for these two classes of migration involved raising the 1975 AHS flow estimates to match the CPR mover estimates in each region. Then these figures were again proportionately adjusted to match

the CPR national flow estimates. The entire adjustment process was repeate
iteratively, matching rows and columns to control totals until an almo
exact match of rows *and* columns was achieved. Successive iteratio
converged to a single solution which was totally consistent with all pu
lished information. It is apparently a unique solution. Movers *from* suburl
were estimated using a similar procedure but only three rows were ma
ched to control totals.

3. City-suburban migration streams are also examined in William H. Fre
   "Black Movement to the Suburbs: Potentials and Prospects for Metr
   politan-wide Integration," Discussion Paper No. 452-77 (Madison: Uni
   ersity of Wisconsin, Institute for Research on Poverty, December 1977
   See also Leo F. Schnore, Carolyn D. Andre and Harry Sharp, "Blac
   Suburbanization, 1930-1970," in *The Changing Face of the Suburb*
   edited by Barry Schwartz (Chicago: The University of Chicago Pres
   1976).

4. For an overview of the impact of migration on metropolitan structure se
   Alden Spear, Sidney Goldstein and William Frey, *Residential Mobilit*
   Migration, and Metropolitan Change (Cambridge, Massachusetts: Ballinge
   1976).

5. Detailed information is available in U.S. Bureau of the Census, *Currer*
   Population Reports, Series P-60, No. 105, "Money Income in 1975 (
   Families and Persons in the United States," and No. 106, "Characteristic
   of the Population Below the Poverty Level: 1975" (Washington, D.C
   U.S. Government Printing Office, both 1977), and in earlier reports.

6. See also, Phoebe H. Cottingham, "Black Income and Metropolitan Re
   idential Dispersion," *Urban Affairs Quarterly*, Vol. 10 (1975), 273-9(

7

Suburban Poverty and Employment Potentials

The prevailing impression is that relatively few living in suburbs are poor, and that those who in fact are poor are not the entrenched poor but rather the young, the elderly and the disabled. The Chapter examines the reality of suburban poverty and assesses the forces which now govern and sustain it. Two facets of the suburban poverty dynamic are isolated for particular attention: first, the impact of migration to and from the suburbs upon the overall magnitude of suburban poverty, and second, the degree to which residence in suburbs heightens the opportunity to secure gainful employment.

The Reality of Black and White Poverty in Suburbs

In 1977, almost one-third of the American black population lived in poverty.[1] At the same time 979,000 blacks, or 20 percent of the total black suburban population, lived below the poverty threshold, while 4,509,000 whites or 6 percent of the total white suburban population, lived in poverty. Consequently, while there were 4.6 times as many suburban whites as blacks in poverty, the proportion of all suburban blacks living in poverty was over three times as high as for whites (Exhibit 12). We find it interesting that during 1959-69, both the black (−21.6 percent) and white (−24.0 percent) levels of

EXHIBIT 12

BLACK AND WHITE POPULATIONS, TOTAL AND BELOW
POVERTY LEVEL, BY RESIDENCE 1959, 1969 and 1977

(Numbers in thousands except percents)

	PERSONS			PERCENT CHANGE[1]	
	1959	1969	1977[4]	1959-69	1969-77
BLACK					
Central Cities[2]	9,636	12,909	13,854	40.0	7.3
Percent in Poverty	40%	24%	29%	−19.4	30.4
Suburbs[3]	2,675	3,433	4,897	28.3	42.6
Percent in Poverty	44%	27%	20%	−21.6	6.0
Nonmetropolitan Areas	6,037	5,714	5,938	− 5.4	3.9
Percent in Poverty	82%	54%	37%	−37.3	−28.3

Notes: 1. The percent change figures corresponding to the rows called "percent in poverty" refer to change in the absolute level of poverty.
2. Central city boundaries for 1977 exclude annexations since 1970.
3. These data refer only to the 243 SMSA's defined in 1970, for all three points in time.
4. The 1977 figures are derived from published data assuming persons per family ratios of: 3.76 (Black), and 3.25 (White).

EXHIBIT 12 (con't)
BLACK AND WHITE POPULATIONS, TOTAL AND BELOW
POVERTY LEVEL, BY RESIDENCE 1959, 1969 and 1977

(Numbers in thousands except percents)

	PERSONS			PERCENT CHANGE[1]	
	1959	*1969*	*1977*[4]	*1959-69*	*1969-77*
WHITE					
Central Cities[2]	49,420	48,909	45,692	− 1.0	− 6.6
Percent in Poverty	13%	10%	10%	−26.8	− 6.6
Suburbs[3]	56,397	70,029	75,155	24.2	7.3
Percent in Poverty	9%	6%	6%	−24.0	7.3
Nonmetropolitan Areas	53,015	56,338	63,245	6.3	12.3
Percent in Poverty	31%	14%	11%	−52.4	−11.8

Source: U.S. Bureau of the Census, *Current Population Reports*, Series P-60, No. 106, Table 4, and Series P-20, No. 116, Table 21 (Washington, D.C.: U.S. Government Printing Office, 1977 and 1978 respectively).

suburban poverty declined at about the same rate, while from 1969
to 1977, the absolute levels of both black and white suburban
poverty rose at about the same rate (6.0 percent black and 7.3
percent white) (Exhibit 12).

Though it is not possible to precisely document the migration of
low-income blacks to suburbs, information is available indicating
levels of migration for family heads receiving "public assistance".[2]
Public assistance is defined to include welfare payments plus other
forms of assistance which may be received by persons not living
below the poverty standard. From 1975 to 1978, 18 percent of the
288,000 black family heads moving to the suburbs from all external
origins received public assistance. At the same time, 35 percent of
the 111,000 black family heads leaving the suburbs during this
period also received public assistance. The result was a net migration
gain of 14,000 black suburban family heads receiving such assistance.
This was the equivalent of just 8 percent of the total net gain of
177,000 black family heads in suburbs due to migration. Consequently, there is occurring a significant increase in black families
residing in suburbs who receive public assistance. It is stressed that
these 14,000 new recipients represent an *increase* above the 73,000
black family head recipients residing in suburbs in 1978 who did not
move between 1975 and 1978.

Suburban Poverty Areas: The Hidden Poor

If income were the prime factor determining the ease with which
blacks could disperse within suburbs, then we might expect that
those having higher incomes could find dwellings in the more prosperous, predominantly white areas most easily. Given the prevalence
of suburban prosperity, we might further expect to find poorer
black households residing at higher densities in less preferred localities. While the evidence regarding the internal configuration of the
black population within suburbs is relatively sparse in the intercensal
years since 1970, some information does exist regarding the population in and outside suburban poverty areas. The suburban "poverty
area" is composed of all census tracts in which over 20 percent of
the population was below the designated low-income level in 1970.
Examining the condition of these tracts within the non-central city
portions of SMSA's in 1977 reveals that 5.4 percent of all suburban
families and 7.3 percent of all unrelated individuals in suburbs live
within them.[3] Of course, not all persons residing within these areas
are living in poverty.

If race played no role in suburban residential patterns, we would
expect that the proportion of poor and non-poor persons living in

overty areas would be the same regardless of race. In fact, however,
his null expectation is not supported by the evidence. In 1977,
mpoverished suburban black families were 3.5 times as likely to
ve in poverty areas as their white counterparts (Exhibit 13). And
uburban unrelated black individuals living alone were 4.9 times
s likely as their white counterparts to live in these same areas.
learly, entry into suburbs does not negate the role of race in res-
lential markets. It is not now possible to establish the relative
ontribution of willful clustering versus discrimination to the current
naping of suburban patterns of race and residence.[4]

Regarding the suburban population living above the poverty
hreshold, it might also be expected that if race were irrelevant,
hen both races would reside in and outside poverty areas in equal
roportions. While the racial differential is here less pronounced,
uburban black families are still 4.8 times as likely to live in poverty
reas as their white counterparts.[5] Note that the racial differential

---

EXHIBIT 13

FAMILIES AND UNRELATED INDIVIDUALS IN SUBURBAN POVERTY
AREAS, BY RACE AND POVERTY STATUS, 1977 [1]

(Numbers in Thousands)

	Above Poverty Level		Below Poverty Level	
	Number	*Percent in Poverty Areas* [2]	*Number*	*Percent in Poverty Areas* [2]
LACK				
Unrelated individuals	358	22	140	44
Families	945	19	225	39
HITE				
Unrelated individuals	5,746	5	1,136	9
Families	20,044	4	963	11
PANISH ORIGIN [3]				
Unrelated individuals	185	12	75	21
Families	801	15	147	27

otes: 1. Families and unrelated individuals in March 1978, by poverty status in 1977.

2. In metropolitan areas "poverty areas" are census tracts in which more than
20 percent of the population was below the poverty level in 1969.

3. Persons of Spanish Origin may be of any race.

ource: U.S. Census Bureau, *Current Population Reports*, Series P-60, No. 116, "Consumer Income: Advance Report" (Washington, D.C.: U.S. Government Printing
Office, July 1978), Table 21.

is actually higher for the non-poverty population than for the poverty population. At the same time, unrelated, non-poverty black individuals living alone in suburbs are 4.4 times as likely as their white counterparts to reside in poverty areas (Exhibit 13).

It might seem a reasonable hypothesis that wealthier black households can move more easily into the more prosperous suburban areas than those in poverty. The evidence suggests this is indeed true. Thirty-nine percent of all suburban black families below the poverty level in 1977 lived in poverty areas, while just 19 percent of all suburban black families above the poverty level lived in such areas (Exhibit 13). A similar differential exists for unrelated black individuals living alone in suburbs and for whites regardless of family stateus. In general, therefore, we have support for the hypothesis that wealthier black households can move more easily into the more prosperous suburban communities than can poorer black households. Of course, not all residential areas outside poverty areas are equally integrated, but no current national data exist examining this point.

Black Suburban Employment Prospects

The prime agent in the transformation of urban America in this century has been the massive but *selective* suburbanization of both jobs and people. As this has occurred, the industrial and occupational structures of metropolitan areas also have been reshaped. The combined effect of spatial transformation and structural shift has been to jar the ladder of upward mobility. All elements of the population, both black and white, have had to adjust to the changing demands and opportunities of the workplace.

A major element of employment change has been the long-run secular shift of the urban economy from an emphasis upon the production of goods to the performance of services.[6] But while all segments of the population have, in a sense, had to contend over several generations with this shift of industrial composition and occupational distribution, blacks have faced a far more severe barrier to suburbanization than whites. At a time when employment opportunities are declining in many central cities, particularly the larger, older ones of the Northeast and North Central regions in which there are large black populations, many central city blacks must seek work in suburbs, and if it is found, some must commute long distances if suburban housing cannot be secured.[7] In addition, many lower income suburban blacks must commute to central city jobs. Clearly, many blacks encounter not only geographic but also institutional barriers in the search for employment.[8]

Much of the growth in national and suburban employment has been in the service-performing industries, and many occupations within these entail the use of specialized skills. While these skills may be learned on the job or in specialized training programs, the years individuals spend in educational institutions is still one effect-ive measure of their employment capacity. Between 1970 and 1975, the mean education level probably rose at a faster rate for blacks than whites, though the black level remains lower than the white (Exhibit 14). Nearly one in five of all suburban blacks eighteen years of age or over who did not move during this period had at least one year of college, and 7.5 percent had college degrees. At the same time over one in five similarly identified whites had attended at least one year of college, and 12.9 percent held college degrees. During this period, net migration between central cities and suburbs led to an increase of 81,000 (37 percent of the black nonmovers having comparable education) in the number of sub-urban blacks having at least one year of college. In addition, there was a net gain of 174,000 suburban blacks having had no college study (18.5 percent of the black nonmovers having comparable education) due to migration between central cities and suburbs. Data regarding education levels for migrants between suburbs and nonmetropolitan areas are not available. In summary, the rate of increase in the number of suburban blacks having at least one year of college study was twice as high as for those with less education during 1970-75 as a result of net migration between central city and suburb, though the absolute increase in those with some college was less than one-half that of those with no college (Exhibit 14).

In suburbs, as almost everywhere else, with few exceptions equal education does not yet insure equal opportunity. One indication of this is the continuing differential between the mean income between blacks and whites at every level of education (Exhibit 14). Though direct comparisions in the aggregate are not wholly appropriate because of differences in age distribution, family status and related characteristics, in 1976 suburban whites having four or more years of college had mean earned incomes which were 45 percent higher than the incomes of blacks comparably educated. Similar differentials exist at all education levels in suburbs and are higher in suburbs than in central cities except for those having four or more years of college. Still, blacks have higher mean incomes in the suburbs than in central cities only in the case of those having eight or fewer years of education or four or more years of college. Whites, on the other hand, have higher mean incomes in the suburbs than in the central cities at all education levels (Exhibit 14). For many blacks, therefore, suburban residence does not guarantee higher earning potential than

EXHIBIT 14
EDUCATION LEVEL OF PERSONS IN, AND MOVING TO AND FROM SUBURBS 1970-75, AND INCOME BY EDUCATION LEVEL IN CENTRAL CITIES AND SUBURBS, 1976

(Numbers in thousands except income)

Race and Years of School Completed	Same House (Nonmovers)		Movers Within And Between SMSA'S		Mean Income of Residents Over 24 Years Having Earnings In 1976 (Dollars)[2]	
	Central Cities	Suburbs[1]	From Central Cities to Suburbs	From Suburbs to Central Cities	Central Cities	Suburbs
WHITE						
Total, 18 years and over	17,313	26,594	6,513	2,607	$8,484	$9,491
Elementary:0-8 years	3,797	4,206	506	189	10,441	11,330
High School: 1-4 years	8,880	14,979	3,267	1,253	12,797	14,076
College: 1-3 years	2,710	3,985	1,293	656	18,726	21,088
4 or more years	1,926	3,424	1,447	509		

Notes: 1. SMSA's are defined as of the 1970 Census. Figures exclude all SMSA's later added. Data for central cities pertain to their 1970 boundaries.
2. Weighted averages.
3. Excludes persons with eight years of education.

(continued on next page)

EXHIBIT 14 (con't)

EDUCATION LEVEL OF PERSONS IN, AND MOVING TO AND FROM SUBURBS 1970-75, AND INCOME BY EDUCATION LEVEL IN CENTRAL CITIES AND SUBURBS, 1976

(Numbers in thousands except income)

Race and Years of School Completed	Same House (Nonmovers)		Movers Within And Between SMSA'S		Mean Income of Residents Over 24 Years Having Earnings In 1976 (Dollars) [2]	
	Central Cities	Suburbs [1]	From Central Cities to Suburbs	From Suburbs to Central Cities	Central Cities	Suburbs
BLACK						
Total, 18 years and over	3,919	1,157	484	265		
Elementary: 0-8 years	1,176	342	62	40	6,355	5,999 [3]
High School: 1-4 years	2,142	598	287	171	7,640	7,910
College: 1-3 years	412	130	71	35	9,639	9,094
4 or more years	180	87	64	19	12,582	14,596

Source: U.S. Bureau of the Census, *Current Population Reports*, Series P-20, No. 285, "Mobility of the Population of the U.S.: March 1970 to March 1975," (Washington, D.C.: U.S. Government Printing Office, October 1975), Table 9; and Series P-23, No. 75, "Social and Economic Characteristics of the Metropolitan and Nonmetropolitan Population: 1977 and 1970" (Washington, D.C.: U.S. Government Printing Office, November, 1978), Table 10.

might exist in central cities. And on the average, it will not insure incomes as high as comparably educated whites. Though college educated suburban blacks earn mean incomes which are just 69 percent of the mean incomes of suburban whites, this differential is exceeded in most other subgroups having less education.[9] In addition, college educated suburban blacks earn, on the average, mean incomes which are greater (by 16 percent in 1976) than their central city counterparts. They therefore may have the greatest incentive to move from central cities to suburbs, and of course, they have the greatest ability to purchase suburban residences. And, of all education subgroups, blacks having college educations are increasing more rapidly in suburbs than most others.

Employment Opportunity and Advancement Potential

Several factors probably work together to diminish black earning potential in suburbs. These include access to employment opportunity and advancement potential within the career tracks associated with given occupations in given industries. Over time of course, workers may break out of one career track to begin another so access and advancement potential intertwine. One dimension of access is geographic, the other institutional. The distribution of suburban commuting distances reflects the combined effect of these two related dimensions.[10]

Geographical Access: Commuting and the Job Search. Blacks encountering discrimination may have to look farther afield to find work. But more distant jobs may be more difficult to discover. At the same time, preferred jobs may be located at a greater distance from predominantly black residential areas than from others. Given the great variety of reasons why black households move to and reside in suburbs, comparisons of commuter distances between central city and suburban black workers in the aggregate might be expected to yield few clear-cut distinctions. Grouping SMSA's by region, however, will make these more useful. In 1975, the fraction of all black central city workers commuting fewer than five miles exceeds the comparable fraction in suburbs in all regions (Exhibit 15). On average, a larger fraction of black suburban workers traveled five or more miles to work than did their central city counterparts. This differential was greatest in the South and West. Variation among regions, of course, would be expected due to differences in the distribution of types and sizes of SMSA's in each as well as differences in central city-suburban income differentials in each region. Also pertinent would be differences among regions in the distribution of black population

EXHIBIT 15

COMMUTING DISTANCES OF BLACK AND WHITE WORKERS RESIDING IN SUBURBS
AND BLACK WORKERS RESIDING IN CENTRAL CITIES, BY REGION, 1975

(Percent distribution by region)[1]

(Residence and Commuting Distance in Miles)[2]	*Northeast* black	white	*North Central* black	white	*South* black	white	*West* black	white
Reside in suburbs								
0 to 4	39	33	32	32	27	31	21	35
5 to 19	31	47	59	49	53	52	60	46
20 or more	30	20	9	19	20	17	19	19
Reside in central cities								
0 to 4	42		36		51		42	
5 to 19	47		52		43		48	
20 or more	11		12		6		10	

Notes: 1. Includes persons working at home, and excludes persons with no fixed workplace.
2. All commuter distances are one-way.

Source: Department of Housing and Urban Development, and the U.S. Bureau of the Census, *Annual Housing Survey, National Public Use Tape, 1975* (Washington, D.C.: Data Users Service Division, Bureau of the Census).

among metropolitan areas. Nevertheless it is somewhat surprising
that black workers residing in suburbs may travel longer distances
to work than do those in central cities. Persons having higher incomes
many of whom are suburban, however, may be more selective
regarding work location and less sensitive regarding commuting cost
if not time.[11]

The meaning of aggregate regional comparisons in the commuting
distances of black and white workers residing in suburbs is also
difficult to interpret. Few national generalizations apply. Only in
the suburbs of the Northeast is the fraction of all commuters
traveling fewer than five miles higher for blacks than whites. But
there also the fraction of all workers residing in suburbs traveling
20 or more miles to work is higher for blacks than whites. Among
all other regions about half of all workers residing in suburbs commute between 5 and 19 miles to work, regardless of race (Exhibit 15).
Here again, differences among regions regarding the internal distribution of types of SMSA's and incomes of residents hamper
analysis.[12]

*Career Tracts: Channeling and Occupational Barriers in Suburban
Employment.* Income advancement in the career tracks of workers
residing in suburbs is strongly influenced by both occupation and
the type of industries in which these occupations are found. While
there is little difference between the occupational distributions of
central cities and suburbs overall *within* racial groups, there is a
substantial difference *between* racial groups. In 1970, just 11 percent
of black employed civilian males sixteen years and over residing in
central cities were employed in professional and managerial occupations combined (Exhibit 16).[13] The comparable figure in suburbs
was 14 percent. In this same year, 61 percent of black males in
central cities were employed as operatives, laborers or service personnel, and 59 percent in suburbs. By comparison, about one-third of
all such white males were employed in the professional-managerial
class in both suburbs and central cities, while just about one-third
were active in the operative-laborer-service class in either place.
Considering only the migration of males sixteen and over who were
employed in 1975, the suburban professional-managerial class
increased due to net migration between central cities and suburbs
by about 65 percent for blacks and only 22 percent for whites
while the operative-laborer-service class increased by 24 percent
for blacks and just 14 percent for whites during 1970-75. Here the
crucial information is the relative shift in black suburban occupational composition due to net migration between central cities and
suburbs. The black male professional-managerial class grew almost
three times as fast as the operative-laborer-service class in suburbs

due to net central city-suburban migration during 1970 to 1975 (Exhibit 16).

The predominant character of the black occupational structure in suburbs is rapidly shifting to the more skilled, higher paying occupations. In an important sense, however, this suggests not only the growing vitality of the black middle class which is increasingly suburban, but also the failure of suburban industry to employ as many black workers in the lower-skill occupations as will be necessary to diminish black poverty in both suburbs and nearby central cities. To some extent this failure is a function of the overall occupational structure of suburban industry, but it also reflects the under-representation of black workers in the lower-skill occupations.[14]

In 1970, only about 4 percent of the non-professional-managerial jobs held by suburban male *residents* were held by blacks, while the suburban population was about 5 percent black. Given the job loss in many of the older central cities having large black populations since 1970, the level at which suburban industry will have to grow to absorb black workers in *metropolitan* areas is substantial. The alternative, of course, is central city revival. In any case, however, many will have to acquire more training and the necessary work habits if they are to garner adequate paying jobs and increase their representation within lower-skill occupations.

Final Comments

This Chapter set out to characterize the suburban poverty dynamic. Two facets of this dynamic were discussed. The first was the impact of migration to and from suburbs upon the magnitude and character of suburban poverty. The second was the manner in which residence in suburbs alters employment potentials.

Migration was determined to be a significant factor in accelerating the suburban poverty rate. During the period from 1975 to 1978, there was a substantial increase in the level of black poverty in suburbs due to the net effect of migration. In this time, however, there were significant flows both to and from the suburban realm. Still, a sizable majority of the volume of net black migration to suburbs in recent years has been above the poverty threshold. Both black families and unrelated individuals living in suburbs were found to be disproportionately concentrated in suburban "poverty areas" whether or not they themselves were impoverished.

Suburban residence would be supposed by many to afford blacks greater employment opportunity than they might have had in the central city. This advantage would be presumed by many to benefit

EXHIBIT 16
NONMOVERS AND MOVERS BETWEEN CENTRAL CITIES AND SUBURBS, BY RACE AND OCCUPATION, FOR EMPLOYED CIVILIAN MALES 16 YEARS AND OVER 1970-75
(Numbers in thousands)

Race and Occupation	SAME HOUSE (Nonmovers)		MOVERS WITHIN AND BETWEEN SMSA'S			
			Absolute Numbers		Percent Distribution[3]	
	Central Cities[1]	Suburbs[2]	From Central Cities to Suburbs	From Suburbs to Central Cities	From Central Cities to Suburbs	From Suburbs to Central Cities
WHITE						
TOTAL EMPLOYED	5,345	9,701	2,593	967	100.0	100.0
Prof., tech., & kindred	826	1,523	605	211	23.3	21.8
Managers	819	1,617	439	150	16.9	15.5
Clerical & kindred	500	679	191	88	7.4	9.1
Sales	408	667	210	83	8.1	8.6
Craft & kindred	1,073	2,117	485	165	18.7	17.1
Operatives	843	1,486	350	133	13.5	13.8
Laborers	325	575	109	54	4.2	5.6
Service	542	752	194	77	7.5	8.0
Farm	8	285	10	5	0.4	0.5

Notes: 1. Central cities according to 1970 boundaries.
2. For SMSA'S defined in the 1970 Census, having 1970 boundaries.
3. Columns may not sum due to rounding.

EXHIBIT 16 (con't)

NONMOVERS AND MOVERS BETWEEN CENTRAL CITIES AND SUBURBS, BY RACE
AND OCCUPATION, FOR EMPLOYED CIVILIAN MALES 16 YEARS AND OVER 1970-75
(Numbers in thousands)

Race and Occupation	SAME HOUSE (Nonmovers)		MOVERS WITHIN AND BETWEEN SMSA'S			
			Absolute Numbers		Percent Distribution[3]	
	Central Cities[1]	Suburbs[2]	From Central Cities to Suburbs	From Suburbs to Central Cities	From Central Cities to Suburbs	From Suburbs to Central Cities
BLACK						
TOTAL EMPLOYED	953	318	174	68	100.0	100.0
Prof., tech., & kindred	56	30	30	10	17.2	14.7
Managers	51	16	11	1	6.3	1.5
Clerical & kindred	77	26	18	3	10.3	4.4
Sales	12	5	4	2	2.3	2.9
Craft & kindred	167	49	36	23	20.7	33.8
Operatives	242	80	31	14	17.8	20.6
Laborers	143	44	28	6	16.1	8.8
Service	201	64	15	9	8.6	13.2
Farm	4	3	2	—	1.1	—

Source: U.S. Bureau of the Census, *Current Population Reports*, Series P-20, No. 285, "Mobility of the Population of the United States: March 1970 to March 1975" (Washington, D.C.: U.S. Government Printing Office, 1975), Table 17.

blacks whether poor or middle class. This advantage has several dimensions. First, it might be asserted that blacks residing in suburbs have a greater opportunity to prepare themselves for gainful employment through access to a variety of support services and as a simple product of an improved living environment. Second, it might be asserted that both the geographic and the social barriers inhibiting job search and career advancement would be far less severe in the suburbs than in the central city.

An appropriate test of these hypotheses would require information regarding the degree to which the income potential of workers increases upon moving to suburbs, relative to the rate at which this potential would have increased had they not moved to the suburbs. This information, however, is not available, at least on a national basis. Consequently, an indirect approach was taken. First, commuting distances between blacks living in central cities and suburbs were examined. On the whole, central city commuting distances were shorter, though it is not possible to control for the types of workplaces to which these commutes delivered the workers. Perhaps more pertinent are the commuting differentials between black and white workers residing in suburbs. Here no clear pattern emerges among major subnational regions. Next, black skill patterns occupational structures and income gradations were examined to assess the ease with which blacks of varying employment capacities would expect to find employment in the suburbs. Some doubt exists regarding the current ability of the types of employers who predominate in suburban regions to employ significant numbers of less-skilled workers, whether black or white.

In summary, the level of black poverty in suburbs is clearly dependent upon two factors: net migration of the poverty population to the suburbs, and the processes by which the suburban milieu transforms the poverty population through access to gainful employment as well as appropriate alternatives for those unable to work. Net migration has contributed significantly to the magnitude of current black poverty in suburbs. This, in itself, is in no sense an indictment of the process of black suburbanization. What is, in fact, more significant is the degree to which residence in suburbs affords individuals an opportunity to rise above the poverty threshold. In this regard, it is not possible to provide direct evidence of success or failure. Suburban employment barriers do indeed seem to be less severe. Geographically, however, blacks residing in suburbs may be somewhat more constrained than whites in securing residence in locations within easy commuting distance of actual or potential work sites. There remains, however, a potential mis-match between

he employment capacities of the low-skill suburban black worker
ind the structure of suburban employment opportunity. The kinds
of jobs they might fill initially are in short supply in some places,
ind those which do exist may be highly dispersed within the suburban realm. This would, in part, account for the relatively long
commuting distances which many black workers residing in suburbs
nake each day. Some of the most prosperous suburban jurisdictions
aave no doubt been accustomed to importing low-skill employees
vho cannot afford the cost of residing in the area, as well.

In any case, the suburban labor market has been shaped by the
evolving interaction between labor supplied and skills demanded.
f the supply of low-skill workers were to increase, then the demand
vould likewise also have to increase if they are to find jobs. In the
hort-run this may not occur. The consequence may be a diminished
ate of net suburban migration of lower-skill black workers. This, in
act, seems to have occurred since the absolute magnitude of in-
migration of lower-skill black workers is far lower than might be
expected, given the large pool of such persons residing in central
ities, and since there has been an appreciable level of out-migration
of such workers in recent years. At this point in time, the cost of
uburban housing and the low rate at which subsidized units are
being constructed are depressing the rate at which the black poor
ind near poor are moving to the suburbs. Many may therefore be
everse-commuting from central city to suburb each day and re-
urning to central city homes at night. Much of the black suburban
ncrease currently occurring is at equilibrium with available employ-
nent opportunities.

NOTES

1. The low-income, poverty threshold is defined by the Federal Interagency
   Committee's poverty index adopted in 1969 and adjusted annually to
   reflect changes in the Consumer Price Index associated with family food
   requirements (by family size and composition, age and sex of head, and
   farm-nonfarm residence) specified in the Department of Agriculture's
   Economy Food Plan. All related data in Exhibit 9 are based solely on
   pre-tax money income excluding certain money receipts such as capital
   gains, but including wages, salaries, Social Security, public assistance
   and welfare, interests, dividends, unemployment compensation, etc.
   All non-money transfers are excluded. For further information see U.S.
   Bureau of the Census, *Current Population Reports*, Series P-60, Nos.
   97 and 98.

2. One person in each family is designated as its "head". A "family" is two
   or more persons related by blood, marriage or adoption residing together.
   A family is receiving "public assistance" if one or more persons in it

received any public assistance or *welfare payments* in the preceding year. Such assistance is defined not to include Supplemental Security Income (SSI) payments. The source of this information is U.S. Bureau of the Census, *Current Population Reports*, Series P-20, No. 331, "Geographical Mobility: March 1975 to March 1978" (Washington, D.C.: Government Printing Office, November 1978). Comparable data for years before 1975 are not available.

3. Only SMSA's which existed in 1970 are here considered, according to the the suburban area they included in that year.

4. At this point in time hard evidence of black attitudes and preferences regarding residential segregation is in short supply. And that which is available tends not to offer a clear indication of the socio-economic correlates or the contextual contingencies of these attitudes and preferences. The anticipation of racial hostility would certainly play a major role in the formation of these preferences, and there may in fact be less discord in some communities having sizable minority populations. There are at least two reasons for this. First, communities having pro-protionately large black populations will necessarily gave proportionately fewer whites. Consequently, a larger share of the daily personal encounters and transactions will be between or among members of the black community. Second, the larger the black relative to the white population, the more accepting may be the white community. This of course is hardly inevitable. The nature of these relations, in any case, would seem to be in many ways influenced by the distribution of power and influence, as well as the derivative attitudes of both respect and self-respect. See De Witt Davis, Jr. and Emilio Casetti, "Do Black Students Wish to Live in Integrated, Socially Homogeneous Neighborhoods?" *Economic Geography*, Vol. 54, No. 3 (July 1978), 197-209. See also, Norman Vieira, "Racial Imbalance, Black Separatism and Permissable Classification by Race," 67 *Michigan Law Review* 1553 (1969); T.F. Pettigrew, "Black and White Attitudes Toward Race and Housing," in *Racial Discrimination in the United States*, edited by T.F. Pettigrew (New York: Harper and Row, 1975), and Brian J.L. Berry, Carole L. Goodwin, Robert W. Lake and Katherine B. Smith, "Attitudes Towards Integration: The Role of Status in Community Response to Neighborhood Change," in *The Changing Face of the Suburbs*, edited by Barry Schwartz (Chicago: University of Chicago Press, 1976), 221-264.

5. Yinger briefly considers racial composition as an amenity factor in residential preference structures and price determination in John Yinger, "The Black-White Price Differential in Housing: Some Further Evidence," *Land Economics*, Vol. 54, No. 2 (May 1978), 187-206, and especially 191-4.

6. For an examination of recent trends in metropolitan employment structure see Thomas A. Clark, "Regional and Structural Shifts in the American Economy Since 1960: The Emerging Role of Service-Performing Industries," in *The American Metropolitan System: Present and Future* edited by Stanley D. Brunn *et al.* (New York: John Wiley and Sons, forthcoming 1979).

7. N.N. Gold, "The Mismatch of Jobs and Low-Income People in Metropolitan Areas and Its Implications for the Center-City Poor," in *Population, Distribution and Policy*, edited by S.M. Mazie (Washington, D.C.:

Commission on Population Growth and the American Future, Research Reports Vol. 5 (1972), 441-486, and John F. Kain, "The Distribution and Movement of Jobs and Industry," in *The Metropolitan Enigma: Inquiries Into the Nature and Dimensions of America's 'Urban Crisis'*, edited by J.Q. Wilson (Cambridge, Massachusetts: Harvard University Press, 1968), 1-43. See also, Pierre De Vise, "The Suburbanization of Jobs and Minority Employment," *Economic Geography*, Vol. 52, No. 4 (October 1976), 348-362, and John R. Logan, "Industrialization and the Stratification of Cities in Suburban Regions," *American Journal of Sociology*, Vol. 82 (September 1976), 333-348.

8. Peter B. Doeringer and Michael J. Piore, *Internal Labor Markets and Manpower Analysis* (Lexington, Massachusetts: Heath-Lexington Books, 1971).

9. Since much of the black suburban population having college educations has arrived only recently in suburbs, and since many of these are younger persons, the black-white suburban income differential may be exaggerated by this statistic. Younger persons are at the early stage of career development and can expect substantial increases in income later in life. The suburban white population having college educations may be somewhat older on average and would tend to have higher incomes as a result.

10. See Michelle J. White, "Job Suburbanization, Zoning and the Welfare of Urban Minority Groups," *Journal of Urban Economics*, Vol. 5 (1978), 219-240. See also, Sanford H. Bederman and John S. Adams, "Job Accessibility and Underemployment," *Annals of the Association of American Geographers*, Vol. 64, No. 3 (September 1974), 378-386; Donald R. Deskins, Jr., "Race, Residence and Workplace in Detroit, 1880 to 1965," *Economic Geography*, Vol. 48 (1972), 79-94; John F. Kain, "Housing Segregation, Negro Employment and Metropolitan Decentralization," *The Quarterly Journal of Economics*, Vol. 82 (1968), 175-197; and Joseph D. Mooney, "Housing Segregation, Negro Employment and Metropolitan Decentralization: An Alternative Perspective," *The Quarterly Journal of Economics*, Vol. 83 (1969), 299-311.

11. The commuting range of lower income black workers is, of course, especially important. Several factors would explain their commuter pattern at any point in time. Central city residents will tend to find work within the central city, though some doubtlessly commute to the suburbs. They may tend to earn less than they would if they had knowledge of and access to the total pool of metropolitan area jobs. For them, longer commuting distances might be indicative of higher wages, though not always. Black central city residents commuting to suburban jobs, of course, may not be able to secure suburban dwellings. For black suburban residents, in turn, commuting distance may be even harder to interpret. Lower income workers here may have longer commuting distances because they must return to the central city to find work. Some, though, may have to travel longer distances to remote suburban workplaces due simply to the geographic pattern of suburban work opportunities. See also, H. Sheppard and A.H. Belitsky, *The Job Hunt* (Baltimore: Johns Hopkins University Press, 1966).

12. When commuting time not distance is examined, a racial differential for suburban residents also exists. Thirty-six percent of all white commuters residing in suburbs and having fixed workplaces had one-way

commutes of 30 or more minutes in 1975, while 44 percent of comparable
black commuters had equivalent commutes. The time differential is only
partly explained by different distance configurations. Mode of travel is
also relevant, but there is little difference between races in the use of the
automobile in commuting in the case of suburban household heads. See
U.S. Bureau of the Census, *Current Housing Reports*, Series H-150-76,
Annual Housing Survey: 1976, Part A (Washington, D.C.: U.S. Government Printing Office, 1978), Tables A-1 and A-6.

13. In this paragraph 1970 estimates and percentage increases are based
exclusively upon the black male population which resided in suburbs
in 1970 and did not move in the ensuing five years.

14. There is apparently a substantial difference in the patterns of occupational
mobility within the life-time career tracks of black and white men in
the nation at large. See Robert M. Hauser and David L. Featherman,
"White-Nonwhite Differentials in Occupational Mobility Among Men
in the United States, 1962-1972," *Demography*, Vol. 11, No. 2 (May
1974), 247-265. See also, Stanley Lieberson and Glenn V. Fuguitt,
"Negro-White Occupational Differences in the Absence of Discrimination,"
American Journal of Sociology, Vol. 73 (1967), 188-200, and U.S. Department of Labor, Bureau of Labor Statistics, *Black Americans: A Decade
of Occupational Change*, Bulletin 1731 (Washington, D.C.: U.S. Government Printing Office, 1972).

8

Suburban Housing Markets and Neighborhoods: A Black Perspective

Interacting Markets: Labor and Housing

Black suburban households, as all others, are positioned at any time in two distinct markets, housing and labor. And the position either will influence the position in the other. Any residential choice pertains not only to the *dwelling unit* itself which is a major element of the household budget but also to a *neighborhood* whose quality will influence housing price, appreciation and human potential, as well as a *location* within the metropolitan geography from which jobs must be sought and resources secured. These residential features will, in turn, influence both the motivation to work and the terms of employment opportunity. The cost of current or desired housing in addition, may influence the number of family members seeking employment. Likewise the location, terms of employment (skill requirements, advancement potential, and the work schedule), and remuneration of the workplace will influence the money income of households and residential preferences regarding location and unit characteristics.

For many of the more prosperous black households now moving to the suburbs, residence *follows* jobs. For the less prosperous, suburbanization may be a more desperate attempt to secure jobs.

Some of these households may arrive with no job, while others may retain jobs in central cities while seeking suburban opportunities.[1] For them, suburbanization may be a staged process involving successive moves to and within suburbs as they jockey for position in both housing and labor markets. This is suggested by the high rates of intra-suburban migration previously noted. For these households, jobs *follow* residence. Of course, many low and moderate income black households are able to secure work in the suburbs while living in the central city. In time many of these subsequently secure suburban dwellings, though not all do so immediately.

Black Housing in Suburbs

The character of suburban dwellings occupied by black households differs in many respects not only in relation to black housing in central cities, but also that of whites in suburbs. Between 1970 and 1976, the number of dwelling units occupied by suburban black households increased by nearly fifty percent. Comparable white units increased in these same years by just 10 percent (Exhibit 17). The proportion of all suburban units occupied by black households which were owned actually fell from 54 to 50 percent, while the percent of white-owned units rose from 65 to 72 percent. These differentials may be indicative only of differences between races in income distribution, however it is more likely that at least some black households elect initially not to purchase homes until they have become more familiar with the opportunities and possible racial barriers within the area. Still others may initially elect to purchase but cannot for various reasons secure desired dwellings.

For reasons previously discussed, the shape and character of black suburbanization has varied significantly among regions of the nation. It is not surprising then that the propensity of blacks to purchase rather than rent suburban dwellings differs significantly from one region to the next as well. In 1976, the rates of home purchase were similarly high in both the North Central (55 percent) and South (54 percent) regions, and low in the Northeast (43 percent) and West (42 percent) (Exhibit 17).

The household's objective in moving from one place to another in the metropolitan area is primarily to improve the match between residential requirements and residential opportunities in light of purchasing power. For whites, this adjustment is played out largely within and among suburbs, but for blacks, this may entail movement from central city to suburb. The differential in black housing opportunity between central city and suburb is indeed substantial.[2] In the nation as a whole in 1975, just 43 percent of black-occupied units in central cities were single-family, while 60 percent of black-occupied units in suburbs were of the same category. These rates, of course, vary substantially among regions (Exhibit 18). Of the units in residential structures containing more than one unit the balance is reversed, with larger proportions in central cities. Mobile homes, thought by many to be one avenue for minority homeownership, apparently play a very minor role in black central city housing and an only slightly greater role in the suburbs, particularly in the Northeast and South (Exhibit 18).[3] Interregional variations in these rates largely reflect differences in central city size distribution and suburban evolution already discussed. They also explain the difference between central cities and suburbs regarding the age of residential structures occupied by black households (Exhibit 18). It is still surprising, however, that fully 42 percent of all suburban black households resided in structures built before 1950. As expected, this group is proportionately best represented in the Northeast and North Central regions where suburbs are perhaps both older and more diverse. This is further evidence of the tendency for suburban blacks to concentrate in the older, inner suburbs.

Black Income-Competitiveness in Purchase and Rental Markets

One indication of the overall competitiveness of black households in suburban housing markets is their income *relative* to white households.[4] Considering mean family incomes, the black-to-white suburban income ratio is comparable among all regions, ranging from a low of 71 percent in the Northeast to a high of just 77 percent in the West (Exhibit 18). When only homeowners are considered, however, the black-to-white mean income ratio rises from a low of 81 percent in the Northeast and to a high of 92 percent in the suburbs of the West. Similar ratios pertaining to suburban renters tend to be lower overall indicating that nearly everywhere, black suburban homeowners are more competitive within the purchase market than black home-renters are in the suburban rental market.[5] Other factors aside, black suburban homeowners would be expected therefore, to somewhat more dispersed than home-renters, within their respective domains of residential choice. In general however, there is probably less dispersion in either group than might be inferred from these data.[6]

Though black suburbanization has proceeded at a remarkable rate over the last decade, it is probable that this rate would have been still higher if it were not for the depressed condition of certain

EXHIBIT 17
CENTRAL CITY AND SUBURBAN HOUSING UNITS,
BY RACE, TENURE, AND REGION, 1976 and 1970
(Numbers in thousands)[1]

| Suburbs | United States | | REGIONS | | | | | | | |
| | | | Northeast | | North Central | | South | | West | |
	1976	1970	1976	1970	1976	1970	1976	1970	1976	1970
BLACK										
Total Occupied Units	1,353	906	255	207	222	148	652	422	223	129
Percent Owned	50	54	43	47	55	59	54	57	42	50
Percent Rented	50	46	57	53	45	41	46	43	58	50
WHITE										
Total Occupied Units	25,826	23,373	6,932	6,316	6,941	5,807	6,077	4,667	5,876	4,585
Percent Owned	72	65	73	72	77	77	72	71	67	64
Percent Rented	28	35	27	28	23	23	28	29	33	36

(continued on next page)

EXHIBIT 17 (con't)
CENTRAL CITY AND SUBURBAN HOUSING UNITS,
BY RACE, TENURE, AND REGION, 1976 and 1970
(Numbers in thousands)[1]

| | United States | | REGIONS | | | | | | | |
| | | | Northeast | | North Central | | South | | West | |
	1976	1970	1976	1970	1976	1970	1976	1970	1976	1970
Central Cities										
BLACK										
Total Occupied Units	4,639	3,823	1,116	1,022	1,324	1,117	1,810	1,390	475	358
Percent Owned	38	35	27	24	42	40	40	39	42	37
Percent Rented	62	65	73	76	58	60	60	61	58	63

Note: 1. In this and all other exhibits appearing below derived from the *Annual Housing Survey,* boundaries are held constant, as defined before March, 1971.

Source: U.S. Bureau of the Census, *Current Housing Reports,* Series H-150-76, "General Characteristics of the U.S. and Regions: 1976," *Annual Housing Survey: 1976, Part A* (Washington, D.C.: U.S. Government Printing Office, 1978), Tables A-1, B-1, C-1, D-1, and E-1.

EXHIBIT 18

GENERAL CHARACTERISTICS OF SUBURBAN AND CENTRAL CITY DWELLING UNITS OCCUPIED BY BLACK HOUSEHOLDS, BY REGION, 1975

(Percentages)

	United States		Northeast		North Central		South		West	
	Central Cities	Suburbs	Central Cities	Suburbs	Central Cities	Suburbs	Central Cities	Suburbs	Central Cities	Suburbs
Units in Structure										
1	43	60	22	44	44	65	54	69	61	58
2-9	34	21	38	31	42	22	28	16	23	22
10 or more	23	17	40	24	14	13	18	11	16	20
Mobile Home	—	2	—	1	—	—	—	4	—	—
Year Structure Built										
Since 1970	6	16	2	10	4	8	10	23	5	18
1950-1969	29	42	22	28	22	42	38	46	38	51
Before 1950	65	42	76	62	74	50	52	31	57	31

EXHIBIT 18 (con't)
GENERAL CHARACTERISTICS OF SUBURBAN AND CENTRAL CITY
DWELLING UNITS OCCUPIED BY BLACK HOUSEHOLDS, BY REGION, 1975
(Percentages)

	United States		Northeast		North Central		South		West	
	Central Cities	Suburbs	Central Cities	Suburbs	Central Cities	Suburbs	Central Cities	Suburbs	Central Cities	Suburbs
BLACK AS PERCENT OF WHITE FAMILY INCOME[1]										
All Families	NA	NA	75	71	81	75	61	73	69	77
In Owned Unit[2]	NA	NA	92	81	95	84	68	80	70	92
In Rented Units	NA	NA	75	82	76	64	66	73	84	79

NA Not available.

Notes: 1. Based on the mean family money income. Family income includes earnings of all persons thirteen years of age and over living in the unit and related to the head.
2. Excludes families in coops and condominiums.

Source: Department of Housing and Urban Development, and the U.S. Bureau of the Census, *Annual Housing Survey, National Public Use Tape, 1975* (Washington, D.C.: Data Users Service Division, Bureau of the Census).

elements of central city housing markets. During the earlier yea
of the 1970's the outmigration of white households from centr
cities was particularly energetic. Many of these households we
homeowners frightened by crime, black "encroachment" and d
clining public services.[7] As a consequence, the effective deman
for homes on the central city purchase market changed shape
black households became more successful in securing discounte
central city residences. Their success is reflected in the 30 percer
increase (from 1.3 to 1.7 million owned units) from 1970 to 197
in the number of central city dwelling units owned by black hous
holds throughout the nation. This amounted to an absolute increas
of 405,000 units.

In these same years (1970-76), the number of suburban uni
owned by black households increased by 190,000 from 490,00
to 680,000 total units (Exhibit 17). In 1976, therefore, there we
2.6 times as many black-owned units in central cities as in th
suburbs. If *all* the increase in homeownership in central cities we
transferred to suburbs, then about 1.1 million homes would hav
been owned by suburban black families instead of the 680,00
which actually were in 1976. In reality, it would have been unlikel
that all the black increase in recent years in central city homeowne
ship could have been transferred to the suburbs. Certainly many c
these households would not have desired to live there. But mor
crucial is the fact that many of these new central city homeowne
could probably not have secured suburban units which would hav
satisfied both their preferences and their pocketbooks. This
because black central city homeowners had lower mean income
than their suburban counterparts.

The reason, in part, that so many black families could purchas
central city homes during 1970-76 was that there was less compe
ition in the form of wealthier, white households.[8] One indicatio
of the higher competitiveness of central city black families is th
black-to-white ratio of mean family incomes in 1975. In that yea
this ratio was actually higher than the comparable suburban ratic
in both the Northeast (92 percent) and North Central (95 percen
regions, while it was lower than the suburban in the South (6
percent) and the West (70 percent) (Exhibit 17). With this in min
it somewhat less surprising to find that the volume of black sul
urbanization was as great as it was in both the South and the We
during the last decade.

Suburban Residential Satisfaction: Rating Houses and Neighborhoods

Despite the high rate of increase in black homeownership in recent years in central cities, it is commonly asserted that there is greater black discontent regarding residential conditions in central cities, and that this is a prime motivation to move to the suburbs. The evidence in fact bears out this assertion. In every region of the nation black respondents queried in the *Annual Housing Survey* indicated greater satisfaction regarding house and neighborhood in suburbs than in central cities. Seven in ten black suburban respondents indicated ratings of "good" or "excellent" for both house and neighborhood, while five or six in ten black respondents in central cities indicated house and neighborhood ratings of "good" or "excellent".[9] Generally there appears to be a significant positive association between these two dimensions of residential satisfaction (Exhibit 19).[10] There is, however, residual variation requiring further study.

Perhaps the most surprising information contained in these preference data is not the substantial differential in residential satisfaction between central city and suburb, but that the overall black ratings of house and neighborhood were as high as they were in the central city. Certainly these ratings are inflated by the recent increase in black central city homeownership, but they are still seemingly high. It is possible that these high ratings in central cities simply reflect limited knowledge of residential alternatives. Still, many central city households have occupied the same unit for relatively long periods of time.

Nationally, 43 percent of all dwelling units occupied by black households in 1975 had been occupied by the same households since at least 1970. In fact 12 percent had been occupied continuously by the same household since at least 1960 (Exhibit 19). Of course, for many this was a condition of poverty not preference, though long residence may breed some measure of commitment to the place of residence. More indicative of central city discontent is the 57 percent of all black central city households residing there in 1975 who had moved since 1970.

Black-White Suburban Housing Differentials

A final point of comparison regards differences between black and white suburban housing. White suburban households, who are about 1.4 times as likely as black households living in suburbs to own their homes, tend on the whole to be more satisfied with house and neighborhood and less mobile than black households. In every

EXHIBIT 19
HOUSE AND NEIGHBORHOOD RATINGS OF BLACK
OCCUPANTS IN CENTRAL CITIES AND SUBURBS, BY REGION, 1975

(Percent distribution)	United States		Northeast		North Central		South		West	
	Central City	*Suburb*	*Central City*	*Suburb*	*Central City*	*Suburb*	*Central City*	*Suburb*	*Central City*	*Suburb*
HOUSING RATING										
Good or Excellent	58	72	50	69	61	74	60	72	64	72
Fair	33	23	36	26	32	20	32	23	30	23
Poor	9	5	14	5	7	6	8	5	6	5
NEIGHBORHOOD RATING										
Good or Excellent	53	73	43	73	50	69	60	74	62	71
Fair	38	24	46	22	39	26	34	22	32	27
Poor	9	3	11	5	11	5	6	4	6	2

EXHIBIT 19 (con't)
HOUSE AND NEIGHBORHOOD RATINGS OF BLACK
OCCUPANTS IN CENTRAL CITIES AND SUBURBS, BY REGION, 1975

(Percent distribution)	United States		Northeast		North Central		South		West	
	Central City	Suburb	Central City	Suburb	Central City	Suburb	Central City	Suburb	Central City	Suburb
YEAR MOVED INTO UNIT										
Since 1970	57	60	54	57	56	55	56	62	65	68
1960-1970	31	24	35	26	31	30	29	18	27	28
Before 1960	12	16	11	17	13	15	15	20	8	4

Source: Department of Housing and Urban Development, and the U.S. Bureau of the Census, *Annual Housing Survey, National Public Use Tape, 1975* (Washington, D.C.: Data Users Service Division, Bureau of the Census).

EXHIBIT 20

COMPARISON OF SUBURBAN DWELLING UNITS OCCUPIED BY BLACK AND WHITE HOUSEHOLDS BY REGION, 1975

(Percentage distributions)

	United States		Northeast		North Central		South		West	
	Black	White	Black	White	Black	White	Black	White	Black	White
Property Value[1]										
$50,000 or more	10	24	11	26	2	21	12	22	13	26
$30,000 to 49,999	28	44	34	49	24	43	23	35	39	47
Under $30,000	62	32	55	25	74	36	65	43	48	27
Mortgage on Property[2]	74	69	74	65	71	69	66	69	99	74
Moved into Unit										
Before 1960	16	21	18	30	15	21	21	16	4	13

Notes: 1. Respondent's estimate of current sale value (house plus lot). One-family homes on less than ten acres, without commercial establishment or medical or dental office on property. Excludes owner-occupied co-ops, condominiums and mobile homes.
2. Percent of all owned units mortgaged.

(continued on next page)

EXHIBIT 20 (con't)
COMPARISON OF SUBURBAN DWELLING UNITS OCCUPIED
BY BLACK AND WHITE HOUSEHOLDS BY REGION, 1975

(Percent distributions)

	United States		Northeast		North Central		South		West	
	Black	White	Black	White	Black	White	Black	White	Black	White
Neighborhood Rating										
Good or Excellent	73	88	73	89	69	90	74	87	71	85
Fair	24	11	22	10	26	9	22	12	27	13
Poor	3	1	5	1	5	.1	4	1	2	2
Units in Structure										
1	60	73	44	70	65	78	69	74	58	71
2-9	21	14	31	21	22	11	16	10	22	14
10 or more	17	9	24	8	13	8	11	11	20	10
Mobile Home	2	4	1	1	—	3	4	5	—	5

Source: Department of Housing and Urban Development, and the U.S. Bureau of the Census, *Annual Housing Survey, National Public Use Tape, 1975* (Washington, D.C.: Data Users Service Division, Bureau of the Census).

region but the South, a greater percentage of suburban white than black households had resided in the same unit since at least 1959, though in all but the West, at least 15 percent of black households residing in suburbs in 1975 had lived in the same unit since at least 1959 (Exhibit 20). Further, on average, the property value (lot plus house) of white-owned suburban homes tended to be appreciably larger than the equivalent for blacks. In the nation as a whole in 1975, for example, 24 percent of all white-owned suburban units were worth $50,000 or more, while just 10 percent of black-owned units fell in this category. At the same time, 62 percent of all black-owned suburban homes were worth less than $30,000, while just 32 percent of white-owned homes entered this class.

Probably less significant is the fact that a higher fraction of black-owned homes were mortgaged than was true of white-owned homes. In 1975, 74 percent of black properties were mortgaged, but only 69 percent of white properties were (Exhibit 20). This differential, which existed in all regions, was undoubtedly due to several factors among which were differences between black and white households regarding length of continuous residence as well as access to sufficient capital to purchase outright. Not surprisingly, black households living in suburbs because of their higher likelihood of renting, are somewhat more likely to live in multi-unit residential structures. In 1975, 38 percent of suburban black households lived in units in structures of two or more units, while just 23 percent of whites did so (Exhibit 20). But since about one-half of all suburban black households resided in rented units at mid-decade while 60 percent lived in one-unit structures, there would appear to be a sizeable class of black single-family home-renters.

Final Comments

The suburban housing market is in fact several distinct but inter-acting markets. Each market segment is composed of a set of places and within these places a set of dwellings differentiated by physical type, tenure, condition and neighborhood. The population of home-seekers is likewise many-dimensioned, and not all have an equal opportunity to participate within the various market segments. Black households, in particular, continue to be excluded from some segments either because they lack access to the social and media circuits which transmit market information, or because they are in other ways discouraged from bidding on available units in exclusive segments. Short of exclusion, there are apparently also occasionally price-penalties which they must pay in order to break into exclusive segments of the suburban housing market.

The effect of racial exclusion and price-penalties is to reduce the extent of the opportunity structure for suburban housing. One consequence may be to channel black demand into particular non-exclusive market segments, and in the process, drive up housing costs in these areas as well. When these non-exclusive housing market segments are geographically clustered, the income-mix within neighborhoods may become far greater than in racially exclusive neighborhoods. One result is that black homeowners may not be able to realize as high a rate of equity accumulation as their white counterparts whose homes may have more extensive resale markets.

Black as well as white households are, at any point in time, positioned in two distinct "opportunity structures": housing and employment. *In many ways these are isomorphic. In each, persons or households search out opportunities (jobs and dwellings), "bid" for position, and secure positions in competitive processes. In addition, once an initial position is secured, its "occupant" will normally seek in time to advance to a more favored position. The crucial fact is that these distinct opportunity structures are interrelated. Not only will the number and type of opportunities in each structure vary over time through mutual interaction within the regional economy, but so also will the positions in each which a household occupies. That is, the position of the worker in the employment structure will influence his housing search space and his competitive standing in the housing market. Likewise, the position of the household in the housing opportunity structure will influence to some degree the job search and the worker's competitive standing in the opportunity structure of the workplace.* When racial discrimination influences the search and competition for housing (or jobs), then the effect will be transmitted to the search and competition for jobs (or housing).

Black suburbanization, therefore, is more than the mere act of securing a suburban residence. It is the process in which blacks gain position in distinct but interacting structures of opportunity. The social order of the suburbs is a product of this complex process. Policymakers would do well to consider the implications of this perspective.

NOTES

1. The role of social networks in securing jobs, and the potential inequities which this may entail in the context of the urban labor market are discussed in H. Sheppard and A.H. Belitsky, *The Job Hunt* (Baltimore: Johns Hopkins University Press, 1966). See also, Paul Bullock, *Aspiration vs Opportunity: Careers in the Inner City* (Ann Arbor, Michigan: Institute of Labor and Industrial Relations, 1973).

2. In many ways it makes more sense to consider central city and suburban characteristics of black-occupied housing instead of the differentials between all housing in these respective places. Blacks have, for long been denied easy access to significant segments of the total housing market. But of course, the character of black suburban housing is changing rapidly as racial and income barriers begin to fall.

3. This impression is corroborated by Richard Smith who found in a study of twelve states that blacks were severely underrepresented in the mobile home market. Possible reasons, he suggests, include residential preference differentials between blacks and whites and racial discrimination in the sale, financing and locating of mobile homes. Richard A. Smith, "An Analysis of Black Occupancy of Mobile Homes," *Journal of the American Institute of Planners*, Vol. 42, No. 4 (October 1976), 410-418.

4. In regard to the income aspect of residential segregation in metropolitan areas see also Phoebe H. Cottingham, "Black Income and Metropolitan Residential Dispersion," *Urban Affairs Quarterly* Vol. 10 (1975), 273-96.

5. There is considerable evidence that race plays a significant role in establishing the price of housing. Courant, for example, demonstrates that segmentation of the urban housing market will arise under a great variety of conditions. Paul N. Courant, "Racial Prejudice in a Search Model of the Urban Housing Market," *Journal of Urban Economics*, Vol. 5 (1978), 329-345. See also, Paul N. Courant and John Yinger, "On Models of Racial Prejudice and Urban Residential Sttucture," *Journal of Urban Economics*, Vol. 4 (1977), 272-291, and A. Thomas King and Peter Mieszkowski, "Racial Discrimination, Segregation, and the Price of Housing," *Journal of Political Economy*, Vol. 81 (1973), 590-606. Additional evidence regarding the effects of both price discrimination and exclusion upon the prices of equivalent units secured by blacks and whites is provided in John Yinger, "The Black-White Price Differential in Housing: Some Further Evidence," *Land Economics*, Vol. 54, No. 2 (May 1978), 187-206. See also, John F. Kain and John M. Quigley, "Housing Market Discrimination, Homeownership, and Saving Behavior," *American Economic Review*, Vol. 62 (June 1972), 263-277.

6. By "dispersion" is meant the distribution of black families within either rented or owned units. Since these units are not uniformily distributed in space, this concept of dispersion is distinct from spatial dispersion. In fact, however, additional insight into the suburban residential process is possible through the examination of racial patterns in suburbs. In this regard, it is observed that in 1970, 39.4 percent of the suburban black population resided in neighborhoods which were in excess of 50 percent black, overall in nonsouthern suburbs. U.S. Bureau of the Census, *Public Use Sample*, Tape Extract, 1970, in Philip Clay, *The Process of Black Suburbanization*, Ph.D. dissertation, MIT Department of Urban Studies and Planning, 1975, p. 199. And, see also Reynolds Farley, "The Changing Distribution of Negroes within Metropolitan Areas: The Emergence of Black Suburbs," *American Journal of Sociology* (January 1970), 512-29.

7. For an incisive examination of the debate surrounding "white flight" see Thomas F. Pettigrew and Robert L. Green, "School Desegregation in Large Cities: A Critique of the Coleman 'White Flight' Thesis," *Harvard Educational Review*, Vol. 46, No. 1 (1976), 1-53.   See also, William H. Frey,

"White Flight and Central-city Loss: Application of an Analytic Migration Framework," Discussion Paper No. 453-77 (Madison: University of Wisconsin, Institute for Research on Poverty, November 1977).

8. While the incomes of black households purchasing homes in central cities may well have been less than many of the white households they replaced, the overall benefit to the central city economy is substantial. Growing black homeownership in central cities is perhaps one of the more significant but neglected trends in urban housing in recent years.

9. See also, David R. Meyer, "Interurban Differences in Black Housing Quality," *Annals of the Association of American Geographers*, Vol. 63, No. 3 (September 1973), 347-352.

10. To examine this association, national cross-tabulations between house score and neighborhood score were generated for black respondents residing in central cities and again for those in suburbs. Generally, the two were positively correlated, indicating either the correlation of the two in "objective" terms, or that the two dimensions tend to merge in subjective evaluations. The latter explanation seems most likely. This analysis employed the *Annual Housing Survey, National Public Use Tape, 1975* (Washington, D.C.: Data Users Service Division, U.S. Bureau of the Census).

9

Age of the house

The Significance and Prospect of Black Suburbanization

The Dichotomy of Black Suburbanization—Middle Class and the Poor

A picture of recent black suburbanization begins to emerge from the data that have been presented. This is a picture of sequence and pattern. Before 1960, 16 percent of the black households now residing in the suburbs already occupied the unit in which they now reside. These households were positioned in the inner, older suburban ring, and in outlying communities, some of which were functionally distinct and not truly "suburban" in character.[1] During the 1960's began the path of continuous, ever more rapid rates of black suburbanization. In this period many more blacks moved to the suburbs, reinforcing old residential patterns while forging inroads in predominantly white suburban communities. Many moved cautiously as legislation and court action opened new opportunities for work and residence.

The 1970's brought rapidly accelerating rates of black suburbanization. This process swept many more to the suburbs, but though the pace was fast, the overall component of the total national black population which was suburban remained almost constant and quite low. In this last decade, the mix of black households arriving in suburbs, either to find better opportunities or to reside nearer suburban workplaces in which household members were already employed, became more diverse regarding family composition, income and residential preference.

The emerging black suburban residential patterns have begun to reflect this growing diversity. More prosperous black households seeking single family residences have probably secured the greatest freedom of suburban movement, though there is evidence this movement is significantly restricted. The less prosperous, if locating without governmental assistance, tend to cluster in the subdistricts of the higher density zones in new or filtered apartments.[2] Others may be drawn to government subsidized units, irregularly positioned throughout the area.

The issue is whether ghetto-like conditions will evolve, replicating central city patterns in the suburban domain. For the more prosperous this seems unlikely, but for the remainder, these conditions already are apparent in suburban "poverty areas", as previously described. Racial succession in individual units in many of these areas is now predominantly white-to-black, or black-to-black. In the suburbs at large during 1967-71, however, just 2.2 percent of white households vacating units were replaced by blacks, while in these same years about 43 percent of black households moving into units replaced whites.[3] It is unlikely that these probabilities of racial succession in residential turnover have varied significantly since the early seventies. Still, these probabilities in all likelihood will differ appreciably among metropolitan areas and different segments of the suburban housing market.[4]

History and Significance: Concluding Observations

The process of black suburbanization is not unlike the arrival of large numbers of southern blacks in northern industrial cities during the first few decades of this century. The black destination was predominantly white, and initial migrants were often scattered throughout the area. In time the receiving cities in these first decades developed patterns of segregation in both work and residence, as the numbers of newly arriving blacks increased to visible proportions.

Today, suburbs are the equivalent racial frontier, but it seems unlikely that their integration will occur in quite the same manner as it did in the central cities of the North and West.[5] For one thing, the geography differs, and for another, the rules of the game have been changed.[6] Today, a far larger fraction of the black suburban population is on an equal footing with the white. For these, the coarser forms of discrimination have been outlawed or lost their effect though it is possible that new, more covert forms will be discovered. For the larger and far less prosperous segment of the black population, however, the condition of suburbanization bears a stronger resemblance to the northern central cities which earlier underwent the process of integration.[7] For them, race and class intertwine, creating opportunities for discrimination which are at least overtly economic.[8]

In the suburbs of the seventies, and soon the eighties, assuming the continuation of both rapid black suburbanization and increasing permanency in the better central city neighborhoods to which blacks have moved and will move, a new superstructure of residential patterns is emerging which will set the tone of race relations for years to come. Wealthier black suburban households will surely find this an encouraging prospect. For the less prosperous, however, there remains considerable uncertainty regarding the form which suburbanization will take.

NOTES

1. See George Sternlieb and W. Patrick Beaton, *The Zone of Emergence: A Case Study of Plainfield, New Jersey* (New Brunswick, N.J.: Rutgers University, Center for Urban Policy Research, 1972); and Solomon Sutker and Sara Smith Sutker (eds.), *Racial Transition in the Inner Suburbs: Studies of the St. Louis Area* (New York: Praeger Publishers, 1974).

2. At issue is whether residential areas in which blacks gain a foothold ultimately will become racial ghettos or, instead, become communities having a relatively stable racial mix. In the past some have posited the existence of racial tipping points not only in neighborhoods but also in schools and other community institutions. See, for example, Eleanor Wolf, "The Tipping-point in Racially Changing Neighborhoods," *Journal of the American Institute of Planners*, Vol. 29, No. 3 (1963), 217-222, and Arthur Stinchcombe, Mary McDill and Dollie Walker, "Is there a Racial Tipping Point in Changing Schools?" *Journal of Social Issues*, Vol. 25, No. 1 (1969), 127-136. Clearly, in the past there is evidence of massive racial transitions in some areas. And clearly, there is necessarily a connection between racial mix and attitudes in both residential areas and associated institutions (workplaces, schools, and the like). But there is no convincing evidence that in the past there has existed a tipping point beyond which will necessarily ensue white flight and rapid racial succession. See John M. Goering, "Neighborhood Tipping and Racial Transition: A Review of Social Science Evidence," *Journal of the American Institute of Planners*, Vol. 44, No. 1 (1978), 68-78. More importantly, there is absolutely no evidence to suggest that massive racial transition, occurring at a pace which accelerates as the proportion black in suburban neighborhoods

increases, will necessarily occur. The determinants of racial mixing are too diverse and varied to produce this result in all places at all times. See James S. Millen, "Factors Affecting Racial Mixing in Residential Areas," in *Segregation in Residential Areas*, edited by Amos H. Hawley and Vincent P. Rock (Washington, D.C.: National Academy of Sciences, 1973). In addition, certain determinants of racial mixing in neighborhoods are amenable to public intervention. These include both short-term initiatives regarding the dwellings themselves (design, location and financing), neighborhood attitudes, receptiveness of ancillary institutions (public and private), as well as the complex of real estate practices which affect the relationship of buyers (or renters) and sellers (landlords). See Harvey Molotch, *Managed Integration: Dilemmas of Doing Good in the City* (Berkeley: University of California, 1972), and Rose Helper, *Racial Policies and Practices of Real Estate Brokers* (Minneapolis: University of Minnesota Press, 1969).

3. See Larry H. Long and Daphne Spain, "Racial Succession in Individual Housing Units," *Current Population Reports*, Special Studies, Series P-23, No. 71 (Washington, D.C.: U.S. Government Printing Office, 1979).

4. See also, Kerry D. Vandell and Bennett Harrison, "Racial Transition among Neighborhoods: A Simulation Model Incorporating Institutional Parameters," *Journal of Urban Economics*, Vol. 5 (1978), 441-470.

5. For examination of alternative future configurations of black residential patterns in metropolitan areas see John F. Kain and Joseph J. Persky, "Alternatives to the Gilded Ghetto," *The Public Interest*, Vol. 14 (1969), 74-87; Anthony Downs, "Alternative Futures for the American Ghetto," *Daedalus*, Vol. 97 (1968), 1331-1378; and David R. Meyer, "Implications of Some Recommended Alternative Urban Strategies for Black Residential Choice," in *Perspectives in Geography 2: Geography of the Ghetto—Perceptions, Problems, and Alternatives* edited by Harold M. Rose (DeKalb: Northern Illinois University Press, 1972), pp. 129-142. Meyer and Downs both offer sets of alternative spatial futures associated with black metropolitan residential patterns. Meyer, for example, suggests five policy clusters: (1) "present" policies, (2) enrichment only, (3) integrated core, (4) segregated dispersal, and (5) integrated dispersal. See also, Matthew B. Edel,"Development or Dispersal? Approaches to Ghetto Poverty," in *Readings in Urban Economics*, edited by Matthew B. Edel and Jerome Rothenberg (New York: Macmillan, 1972).

6. Thomas Lee Philpott, *The Slum and the Ghetto: Neighborhood Deterioration and Middle-class Reform, Chicago, 1880-1930* (New York: Oxford University Press, 1978).

7. Furthermore, it is now contended by many that the black experience in the major northern industrial cities has been profoundly different from that of the other ethnic groups which have emerged into American society through the assimilative processes of the city. See for example, Theodore Hershberg, *et al.*, "A Tale of Three Cities: Blacks and Immigrants in Philadelphia: 1850-1880, 1930 and 1970," *The Annals of the American Academy of Political and Social Science*, (January 1979). See also Stephen Thernstrom, *The Other Bostonians: Poverty and Progress in the American Metropolis* (Cambridge, Massachusetts: Harvard University Press, 1973). Chapter 10, "Blacks and Whites".

8. For a recent examination of this theme see William J. Wilson, *The Declining Significance of Race: Blacks and Changing American Institutions* (Chicago: University of Chicago Press, 1979). See also, L.F. Schnore, *Class and Race in Cities and Suburbs* (Chicago: Markham Publishing Company, 1972); and Otis D. Duncan, "Inheritance of Poverty or Inheritance of Race," in *On Understanding Poverty*, edited by D.P. Moyniham (New York: Basic Books, 1969).

Bibliography

Black Suburbanization as a Spatial Process

Clark, W.A.V. "Patterns of Black Intraurban Mobility and Restricted Relocation Opportunities," in *Perspectives in Geography 2: Geography of the Ghetto* (edited by Harold M. Rose). DeKalb: Northern Illinois University Press, 1972.

Clay, Phillip. *The Process of Black Suburbanization*. Ph.D. dissertation, MIT Department of Urban Studies and Planning, 1975.

Connally, Harold X. "Black Movement to the Suburbs: Suburbs Doubling Their Black Populations During the 1960's," *Urban Affairs Quarterly*, Vol. 9 (1973), 91-111.

Delaney, P. "Negroes Find Few Tangible Gains," in *Suburbia in Transition* (edited by L.H. Masotti and J.K. Hadden) New York: New Viewpoints for the New York Times, 1974, 278-82.

Farley, Reynolds. "The Changing Distribution of Negroes within Metropolitan Areas: The Emergence of Black Suburbs," *American Journal of Sociology*, Vol. 75 (1970), 512-29.

Frey, William H. "White Flight and Central-city Loss: Application of an Analytic Migration Framework," Discussion Paper No. 453-77, Madison: University of Wisconsin, Institute for Research on Poverty, November 1977.

Frieden, Bernard J. "Blacks in Suburbia: The Myth of Better Opportunities," in *Minority Perspectives*. (Series editor, L.Wingo). Baltimore: Johns Hopkins University Press, For Resources for the Future, Inc., The Governance of Metropolitan Regions No. 2, 1972, 31-49.

Grier, Eunice and George Grier. "Black Suburbanization at the Mid-1970's," Washington, D.C.: Washington Center for Metropolitan Studies, April 1978.

Hershberg, Theodore, *et al.* "A Tale of Three Cities: Blacks and Immigrants in Philadelphia: 1850-1880, 1930 and 1970," *The Annals of the American Academy of Political and Social Science*, January 1979.

Long, Larry H. "How the Racial Composition of Cities Changes," *Land Economics*, Vol. LI, No. 3 (August 1975), 258-67.

McAllister, Ronald J., Edward J. Kaiser and Edgar W. Butler. "Residential Mobility of Blacks and Whites: A National Longitudinal Survey," *American Journal of Sociology* Vol. 77 (1972), 445-55.

Morrill, Richard. "The Negro Ghetto: Problems and Alternatives," *Geographical Review*, Vol. 55 (1965), 339-61.

————. "A Geographic Perspective of the Black Ghetto," in *Perspectives in Geography 2: Geography of the Ghetto* (edited by Harold M. Rose) DeKalb: Northern Illionis University Press, 1972.

Rabinovitz, Francine F. and William J. Siembieda. *Minorities in Suburbs: The Los Angeles Experience*. Lexington, Massachusetts: Lexington Books, 1977.

Rose, Harold. "Development of an Urban Sub-system: The Case of the Negro Ghetto," *Annals of the Association of American Geographers*, Vol. 60 (1970), 1-17.

————. "The All-Black Town: Suburban Prototype or Rural Slum?"in *People and Politics in Urban Society* (edited by Harlan Haber). Beverly Hills, California: Sage Publications, Inc., 1972, 397-431.

———— *Black Suburbanization: Access to Improved Quality of Life or Maintenance of the Status Quo?*. Cambridge, Massachusetts: Ballinger, 1976.

Roseman, Curtis C. and Prentice Knight. "Residential Environment and Migration Behavior of Urban Blacks," *The Professional Geographer*, Vol. XXVII, No. 2 (May 1975), 160-65.

Schnare, Ann B. *Residential Segregation by Race in U.S. Metropolitan Areas: An Analysis Across Cities and Over Time*. Washington, D.C.: The Urban Institute, February 1977.

Schnore, Leo F., Carolyn D. Andre, and Harry Sharp. "Black Suburbanization, 1930-1970," in *The Changing Face of the Suburbs* (edited by Barry Schwartz). Chicago: The University of Chicago Press, 1976.

Sorenson, Annemette, Karl E. Taeuber, and Leslie J. Hollingsworth. "Indexes of Racial Residential Segregation for 109 Cities in the United States, 1940 to 1970," *Sociological Focus* (April 1975), 125-42.

Spear, Alden, Sidney Goldstein, and William Frey. *Residential Mobility, Migration, and Metropolitan Change*. Cambridge, Massachusetts: Ballinger, 1976.

Sternlieb, George and W. Patrick Beaton. *The Zone of Emergence: A Case Study of Plainfield, New Jersey.* New Brunswick, N.J.: Rutgers University, Center for Urban Policy Research, 1972.

Taeuber, Karl E. "Racial Segregation: The Persisting Dilemma," *Annals of the American Academy of Political and Social Science* (November 1975), 87-96.

———— and Alma F. Taeuber. *Negroes in Cities: Residential Segregation and Neighborhood Change.* Chicago: Aldine Publishing Company, 1965.

Thernstrom, Stephan. *The Other Bostonians: Poverty and Progress in the American Metropolis.* Cambridge, Massachusetts: Harvard University Press, 1973.

Residential Filtering, Neighborhood Change and the Socio-Institutional Dynamics of Succession

Berry, Brian J.L., Carole L. Goodwin, Robert W. Lake and Katherine B. Smith. "Attitudes Towards Integration: The Role of Status in Community Response to Neighborhood Change," in *The Changing Face of the Suburbs* (edited by Barry Schwartz). Chicago: University of Chicago Press, 1976, 221-64.

Courant, Paul N. and John Yinger. "On Models of Racial Prejudice and Urban Residential Structure," *Journal of Urban Economics*, Vol. 4 (1977), 272-91.

Davis, De Witt, Jr. and Emilio Casetti. "Do Black Students Wish to Live in Integrated, Socially Homogeneous Neighborhoods?" *Economic Geography*, Vol. 54, No. 3 (July 1978), 197-209.

Goering, John M. "Neighborhood Tipping and Racial Transition: A Review of Social Science Evidence," *Journal of the American Institute of Planners*, Vol. 44, No. 1 (1978), 68-78.

Lansing, John B., Charles W. Clifton, and James N. Morgan. *New Homes and Poor People: A Study of Chain Moves.* Ann Arbor, Michigan: University of Michigan, Institute for Social Research, 1969.

Long, Larry H. and Daphne Spain. "Racial Succession in Individual Housing Units," *Current Population Reports*, Special Studies, Series P-23, No. 71. Washington, D.C.: U.S. Government Printing Office, 1979.

Millen, James S. "Factors Affecting Racial Mixing in Residential Areas," in *Segregation in Residential Areas* (edited by Amos H. Hawley and Vincent P. Rock). Washington, D.C.: National Academy of Sciences, 1973.

Norwood, L.K. and E.A.T. Barth. "Urban Desegregation: Negro Pioneers and Their White Neighbors," in *End of Innocence: A Suburban Reader* (edited by C.M. Haar). Glenview, Illinois: Scott, Foresman, 1972, 118-23.

Pettigrew, Thomas F. "Black and White Attitudes Toward Race and Housing," in *Racial Discrimination in the United States* (edited by T.F. Pettigrew). New York: Harper and Row, 1975.

———— and Robert L. Green. "School Desegregation in Large Cities: A Critique of the Coleman 'White Flight' Thesis," *Harvard Educational Review*, Vol. 46, No. 1 (1976), 1-53.

Smith, Wallace F. *Filtering and Neighborhood Change*, Research Report No. 24. Berkeley: The University of California, The Center for Real Estate and Urban Economics, Institute of Urban and Regional Development, 1964.

Stinchcombe, Arthur, Mary McDill and Dollie Walker. "Is there a Racial Tipping Point in Changing Schools?" *Journal of Social Issues*, Vol. 25, No. 1 (1969) 127-36.

Sutker, Solomon and Sara Smith Sutker (eds.). *Racial Transition in the Inner Suburb: Studies of the St. Louis Area.* New York: Praeger Publishers, 1974.

Vandell, Kerry D. and Bennett Harrison. "Racial Transition among Neighborhoods: A Simulation Model Incorporating Institutional Parameters," *Journal of Urban Economics*, Vol. 5 (1978), 441-70.

Vieira, Norman. "Racial Imbalance, Black Separatism and Permissible Classification by Race," 67 *Michigan Law Review* 1553 (1969).

Wolf, Eleanore. "The Tipping-point in Racially Changing Neighborhoods," *Journal of the American Institute of Planners*, Vol. 29, No. 3 (1963), 217-22.

Exclusionary Practices

Bergman, E.M. *Eliminating Exclusionary Zoning: Reconciling Workplace and Residence in Suburban Areas.* Cambridge, Massachusetts: Ballinger, 1974.

Finkler, Earl, *et al. Urban Nongrowth.* New York: Praeger, 1976.

Fishman, Richard P. (ed.). *Housing For All Under Law: New Directions in Housing, Land Use and Planning Law—A Report of the American Bar Association's Advisory Commission on Housing and Urban Growth.* Cambridge, Massachusetts: Ballinger, 1978.

Foley, Donald. "Institutional and Contextual Factors Affecting the Housing Choices of Minority Residents," in *Segregation in Residential Areas* (edited by Amos H. Hawley and Vincent P. Rock). Washington D.C.: National Academy of Sciences, 1973; reprinted in *The Manipulated City: Perspectives on Spatial Structures and Social Issues in Urban America* (edited by S. Gale and E.G. Moore). Chicago: Maaroufa Press, 1975, 168-81.

Helper, Rose. *Racial Policies and Practices of Real Estate Brokers.* Minneapolis: University of Minnesota Press, 1969.

Hughes, James W. "Dilemmas of Suburbanization and Growth Controls," *Annals of the American Academy of Political and Social Science*, (1975), 422: 61-76.

Palm, Risa. *Urban Social Geography from the Perspective of the Real Estate Salesman.* Berkeley: Center for Real Estate and Urban Economics, University of California, Research Report No. 38, 1976.

——. "Spatial Segmentation of the Urban Housing Market," *Economic Geography*, Vol. 54, No. 3 (July 1978), 210-21.

Pearlman, Kenneth. "The Closing Door: The Supreme Court and Residential Segregation," *Journal of the American Institute of Planners*, Vol. 44, No. 2 (April 1978), 160-69.

Rose, Jerome G. *After Mount Laurel: The New Suburban Zoning*. New Brunswick: Rutgers University, Center for Urban Policy Research, 1977.

Employment, Occupational Structure and Income

Bederman, Sanford H. and John S. Adams. "Job Accessibility and Underemployment," *Annals of the Association of American Geographers*, Vol. 64, No. 3 (September 1974), 378-86.

Bullock, Paul. *Aspiration vs. Opportunity: "Careers" in the Inner City*. Ann Arbor, Michigan: Institute of Labor and Industrial Relations, 1973.

Clark, Thomas A. "Regional and Structural Shifts in the American Economy Since 1960: The Emerging Role of Service-Performing Industries," in *The American Metropolitan System: Present and Future* (edited by Stanley D. Brunn *et al.*). New York: John Wiley and Sons, forthcoming 1979.

Cottingham, Phoebe H. "Black Income and Metropolitan Residential Dispersion," *Urban Affairs Quarterly*, Vol. 10 (1975), 273-96.

Deskins, Donald R., Jr. "Race, Residence and Workplace in Detroit, 1880-1965," *Economic Geography*, Vol. 48 (1972), 79-94.

De Vise, Pierre. "The Suburbanization of Jobs and Minority Employment," *Economic Geography*, Vol. 52, No. 4 (October 1976), 348-62.

Doeringer, Peter B. and Michael J. Piore. *Internal Labor Markets and Manpower Analysis*. Lexington, Massachusetts: Heath-Lexington Books, 1971.

Gold, N.N. "The Mismatch of Jobs and Low-Income People in Metropolitan Areas and Its Implications for the Center-City Poor," in *Population, Distribution and Policy* (edited by S.M. Mazie). Washington, D.C.: Commission on Population Growth and the American Future, Research Reports Vol. 5 (1972), 441-86.

Hauser, Robert M. and David L. Featherman. "White-Nonwhite Differentials in Occupational Mobility Among Men in the United States, 1962-1972," *Demography*, Vol. 11, No. 2 (May 1974), 247-65.

Haveman, Robert. "Poverty, Income Distribution and Social Policy: The Last Decade and the Next," Discussion Paper No. 365-76. Madison: University of Wisconsin, Institute for Research on Poverty, 1976.

Hill, Robert B. "The Illusion of Black Progress," *Social Policy*, (November/December 1978), 14-25.

Jencks, Christopher, *et al. Inequality: A Reassessment of the Effect of Family and Schooling in America*. New York: Basic Books, 1972.

Kain, John F. "The Distribution and Movement of Jobs and Industry," in *The Metropolitan Enigma: Inquiries Into the Nature and Dimensions of America's 'Urban Crisis'* (edited by J.Q. Wilson). Cambridge, Massachusetts: Harvard University Press, 1968, 1-43.

———. "Housing Segregation, Negro Employment and Metropolitan Decentralization," *Quarterly Journal of Economics*, Vol. 82 (1968), 175-97.

Lieberson, Stanley and Glenn V. Fuguitt. "Negro-White Occupational Differences in the Absence of Discrimination," *American Journal of Sociology*, Vol. 73 (1967), 188-200.

Logan, John R. "Industrialization and the Stratification of Cities in Suburban Regions," *American Journal of Sociology*, Vol. 82 (September 1976), 333-48.

Masters, S.H. *Black-White Income Differentials: Empirical Studies and Policy Implications.* New York: Academic Press, Research on Poverty Monograph Series, 1975.

Mooney, Joseph D. "Housing Segregation, Negro Employment and Metropolitan Decentralization: An Alternative Perspective," *The Quarterly Journal of Economics*, Vol. 83 (1969), 299-311.

Plotnik, Robert and Felicity Skidmore. *Progress Against Poverty: A Review of the 1964-74 Debate.* New York: Academic Press, 1975.

Ravitch, Diane. "60's Education, 70's Benefits," *New York Times* (June 29, 1978).

Sheppard, H. and A.H. Belitsky. *The Job Hunt.* Baltimore: Johns Hopkins Press, 1966.

Smith, James P. and Finis R. Welch. "Race Differences in Earnings: A Survey and New Evidence," R-2295-NSF (Santa Monica, California: RAND Corporation, 1978).

U.S. Department of Labor, Bureau of Labor Statistics. *Black Americans: A Decade of Occupational Change.* Bulletin 1731. Washington, D.C.: U.S. Government Printing Office, 1972.

White, Michelle, J. "Job Suburbanization, Zoning and the Welfare of Urban Minority Groups," *Journal of Urban Economics*, Vol. 5 (1978), 219-40.

Racial Dimensions of Urban Housing Markets

Berry, B.J.L. and R.S. Bednarz. "A Hedonic Model of Prices and Assessments for Single-Family Homes: Does the Assessment Follow the Market or the Market Follow the Assessor?" *Land Economics* Vol. 51 (1975), 21-40.

Courant, Paul N. "Racial Prejudice in a Search Model of the Urban Housing Market," *Journal of Urban Economics*, Vol. 5 (1978), 329-45.

Eggers, Frederick J., *et al.* "Background Information and Initial Findings of the Housing Market Practices Survey," Washington, D.C.: U.S. Department of Housing and Urban Development, April 17, 1978.

Haar, C.M. and D.S. Iatridis. *Housing the Poor in Suburbia: Public Policy at the Grass Roots.* Cambridge, Massachusetts: Ballinger, 1974.

Kain, John F. and John M. Quigley. "Housing Market Discrimination, Home-ownership, and Saving Behavior," *American Economic Review*, Vol. 62 (June 1972), 263-77.

————. *Housing Markets and Racial Discrimination: A Microeconomic Analysis* New York: National Bureau of Economic Research, 1975.

Kilborn, Peter T. "Corporate Giants Invade the Residential Market," *New York Times*, February 4, 1979.

King, A. Thomas and Peter Mieszkowski. "Racial Discrimination, Segregation, and the Price of Housing," *Journal of Political Economy*, Vol. 81 (1973), 590-606.

Meyer, David R. "Interurban Differences in Black Housing Quality," *Annals of the Association of American Geographers*, Vol. 63, No. 3 (September 1973), 347-52.

Rubinowitz, L.S. *Low-Income Housing: Suburban Strategies*. Cambridge, Massachusetts: Ballinger, 1974.

Schnare, A.B. and R.J. Struyk. "Segmentation in Urban Housing Markets," *Journal of Urban Economics*, Vol. 3 (1976), 146-66.

Smith, Richard A. "An Analysis of Black Occupancy of Mobile Homes," *Journal of the American Institute of Planners*, Vol. 42, No. 4 (October 1976), 410-18.

Yinger, John. "The Black-White Price Differential in Housing: Some Further Evidence," *Land Economics*, Vol. 54, No. 2 (May 1978), 187-206.

Political Dimensions of Black Suburbanization

Danielson, M.N. "Differentiation, Segregation, and Political Fragmentation in the American Metropolis," in *Governance and Population* (edited by A.E.K. Nash). Washington, D.C.: Commission on Population Growth and the American Future, Research Reports, Vol. 4, 1972, 143-76.

Fainstein, Norman and Susan Fainstein. *Urban Political Movements: The Search for Power by Minority Groups in American Cities*. Englewood Cliffs, New Jersey: Prentice-Hall, 1974.

Friesma, H. Paul. "Black Control of Central Cities: The Hollow Prize," *Journal of the American Institute of Planners*, Vol. 35 (1969), 75-9.

Greenstone, J.David and Paul E. Peterson. *Race and Authority in Urban Politics: Community Participation and the War on Poverty*. New York: Russell Sage Foundation, 1973.

Philpott, Thomas Lee, *The Slum and the Ghetto: Neighborhood Deterioration and Middle Class Reform, Chicago, 1880-1930*. New York: Oxford University Press, 1978.

Piven, Frances Fox and Richard A. Cloward. "Black Control of Cities," *The New Republic*, September 30 and October 7, 1967.

Regional Geographic Distribution of the Black Population

Calef, Wesley C. and Howard J. Nelson. "Distribution of Negro Population in the United States," *Geographical Review*, Vol. 46, No. 1 (January, 1956).

Evans, Eli. "The City, South and Caribbean (II)," *New York Times* (June 27, 1978).

Hart, John Fraser. "The Changing Distribution of the American Negro," *Annals Association of American Geographers*, Vol. 50, No. 3 (September 1960), 242-66.

Long, Larry. United States Bureau of the Census, "Interregional Migration of the Poor: Some Recent Changes," *Current Population Reports*, Series P-23, No. 73. Washington, D.C.: Government Printing Office, 1978.

Smith, T.Lynn. "The Redistribution of the Negro Population of the United States, 1910-1960," *The Journal of Negro History*, Vol. LI, No. 3 (July 1966), 155-73.

Alternative Futures: Race, Residence and the Social Order of the Urban Region

Bell, D.A. "Affirmative Discrimination: Ethnic Inequality and Public Policy— A Review of Glazer," *Emory Law Journal*, Vol. 25 (February 1976).

Downs, Anthony. "Alternative Futures for the American Ghetto," *Daedalus*, Vol. 97 (1968), 1331-78.

———. *Opening Up the Suburbs*. New Haven: Yale University Press, 1973.

Duncan, Otis D. "Inheritance of Poverty or Inheritance of Race," in *On Understanding Poverty* (edited by D.P. Moynihan). New York: Basic Books, 1969.

Edel, Matthew B. "Development or Dispersal? Approaches to Ghetto Poverty," in *Readings in Urban Economics* (edited by Matthew B. Edel and Jerome Rothenberg). New York: Macmillan, 1972.

Frey, William H. "Black Movement to the Suburbs: Potentials and Prospects for Metropolitan-wide Integration," Discussion Paper No. 452-77. Madison: University of Wisconsin, Institute for Research on Poverty, December 1977.

Glazer, Nathan. "On 'Opening Up' the Suburbs," *Public Interest*, Vol. 37 (1974), 89-111.

———. *Affirmative Discrimination: Ethnic Inequality and Public Policy*. New York: Basic Books, 1975.

Gross, Barry R. *Discrimination in Reverse: Is Turnabout Fair Play?* New York: New York University Press, 1978.

Harrison, Bennett. *Urban Economic Development: Suburbanization, Minority Opportunity and the Condition of the Central City*. Washington, D.C.: The Urban Institute, 1974.

Harvey, David. "The Political Economy of Urbanization in the Advanced Capitalist Countries: The Case of the U.S." in the *Urban Affairs Annual Review*. Beverley Hills: Sage Publications, 1975.

———. "Revolutionary and Counter-Revolutionary Theory in Geography, and the Problem of Ghetto Formation," in *Perspectives in Geography 2: The Geography of the Ghetto—Perceptions, Problems, and Alternatives* (edited by Harold M. Rose). DeKalb: Northern Illinois University Press, 1972, 2-25.

Hirsch, Fred. *Social Limits to Growth*. Cambridge: Harvard University Press, 1976.

Kain, John F. and Joseph J. Persky. "Alternatives to the Guilded Ghetto," *The Public Interest*, Vol. 14 (1969), 74-87.

Listokin, David. *Fair Share Housing Allocation*. New Brunswick: Rutgers University, Center for Urban Policy Research, 1976.

Meyer, David R. "Implications of Some Recommended Alternative Urban Strategies for Black Residential Choice," in *Perspectives in Geography 2: Geography of the Ghetto—Perceptions, Problems, and Alternatives* (edited by Harold M. Rose). DeKalb: Northern Illinois University Press, 1972, 129-42.

Miller, David. *Social Justice*. New York: Oxford University Press, 1976.

Molotch, Harvey. *Managed Integration: Dilemmas of Doing Good in the City*. Berkeley: University of California, 1972.

Schnore, L.F. *Class and Race in Cities and Suburbs*. Chicago: Markham Publishing Company, 1972.

Wilson, William J. *The Declining Significance of Race: Blacks and Changing American Institutions*. Chicago: University of Chicago Press, 1979.

Index*

*Page number followed by "n" denotes footnote. Italicized subjects are major concepts. All author citations are in footnotes unless otherwise indicated.